Boutique Bean Pot

Other Books by Kathleen Mayes

The Sodium-Watcher's Guide
Osteoporosis: Brittle Bones and the Calcium Crisis
Fighting Fat!
The Complete Guide to Digestive Health
Beat Jet Lag

Boutique Bean Pot

*Exciting Bean Varieties
in Superb New Recipes*

Kathleen Mayes
Sandra Gottfried

Woodbridge Press
Santa Barbara, California 93160

Published and Distributed by

Woodbridge Press Publishing Company
Post Office Box 6189
Santa Barbara, California 93160

Distributed simultaneously in the United States and Canada.
Printed in the United States of America.

Library of Congress Cataloging-in-publication Data

Mayes, Kathleen.
    Boutique bean pot : exciting bean varieties in delicious new recipes / Kathleen Mayes, Sandra Gottfried.
        p. cm.
    Includes bibliographical references and indexes.
    ISBN 0-88007-196-6 : $12.95
    1. Cookery (Beans) I. Gottfried, Sandra. II. Title.
TX803.B4M39   1992
641.6′565--dc20   92-7572
                                                          CIP

Cover illustrations: *Janice Blair*

Note to the Reader

The information in this book is for general information and no responsibility is assumed on the part of the authors or the publishers for its application or use in any specific case or by any particular person.

It is not the purpose of this publication to replace the services of a physician, nor to guarantee any nutritional or medicinal preparation or the effectiveness thereof. This information is not presented with the intention of diagnosing or prescribing.

Before beginning any change in diet or exercise, it is recommended that you consult your doctor or other health professional. If you are on a special diet under the direction of your doctor or other health professional, it is important to follow their instructions.

Any use of brand names in this guide is for identification only, and does not imply endorsement or otherwise by the authors.

Contents

List of Illustrations

Figure:

Color Plates: (Insert follows Page 16)

Acknowledgments

The authors warmly acknowledge the invaluable assistance and cooperation given by many people in connection with this guide. We want particularly to thank Ken Rauch of The Bean Bag, Oakland, California, Valerie Phipps of Phipps Ranch, Pescadero, California, and Philip Teverow of Dean and DeLuca, New York City, for their wonderful help. Special thanks also go to:

Adobe Milling Company, Inc., Dove Creek, Colorado
AkPharma, Inc., Pleasantville, New Jersey
American Dry Bean Board, Scottsbluff, Nebraska
Arrowhead Mills, Inc., Hereford, Texas
Buckeye Beans and Herbs, Spokane, Washington
California Dry Bean Advisory Board, Dinuba, California
Colorado State University, Fort Collins, Colorado
Good Taste, Ketchum, Idaho
Idaho Bean Commission, Boise, Idaho
Michigan Bean Shippers Association, Saginaw, Michigan
National Dry Bean Council, Saginaw, Michigan
Native Seeds/SEARCH, Tucson, Arizona
Northarvest Bean Growers Association, Frazee, Minnesota
Peas, Inc., Pleasanton, Texas
USA Dry Pea & Lentil Council, Moscow, Idaho
Vermont Bean Seed Company, Fair Haven, Vermont
Western Bean Dealers Association, Inc., Twin Falls, Idaho

Graphics Credits

Color plates 1 to 13: original photographs by Terry Mayes, Arlington, Texas. Color plates 14, 15, 17 to 24: reproduced by kind permission of the Idaho Bean Commission, Boise, Idaho. Drawings and tables: Sigma Graphics, Santa Barbara, California.

CHAPTER 1

Introducing the World of New Beans

Welcome to the world of *new* beans!

At first glance, beans may seem rather dull, because many Americans are only acquainted with baked beans, refried beans, three-bean salad and chili. Boring. While other cultures and other countries around the world have never stopped regarding dried beans as staples in the kitchen, Americans forgot them—until recently.

Fresh excitement is simmering in the cooking world with the rediscovery of legumes—dried beans, peas and lentils—and their newly-found benefits. Beans are now staging a full-scale and upscale comeback to the vegetarian scene, and the improved availability of many unusual varieties is creating increased enthusiasm. Beans are worth knowing.

Happy travelers

Beans that were once considered rare are showing up in health-food stores and specialty markets. We can now share in the enjoyment of beans that formerly were separated by culture or geography—varieties from the South can be bought in Northern states, Western beans can now be relished on the East Coast.

You may be familiar with the pinto—but do you know the Appaloosa or Jacob's Cattle? You may know the Great Northern—but have you seen the wonderful Snowcap? You may have cooked up a pot of black beans, but have you tried Black Valentines? You have treats in store!

Unusual kinds (Appendix 1 identifies more than seventy) come to us in different ways, many being imported: greater supplies are becoming available of such beans as Japanese adzukis, Indian dals and nuñas, the popping beans from South America. At the same time, lesser-known U.S. selections are reappearing after having been carefully preserved by eager seed savers, small-scale commercial growers and Native Americans of the Southwest who had treasured "heirlooms" for their particular characteristics of shape, texture and taste. In addition, other varieties are being introduced by way of recent successes in U.S. plant technology: an expansion in research is finding not only which beans grow best in certain types of soil and climate, but creating a whole new world of "boutique" beans with a riot of shapes, colors and flavors that give fresh sparkle to dishes and menus, and that cook quickly when you are short of time or want to prepare them on the spur of the moment.

A full spectrum of colors and flavors

The natural colors are dazzling: there are white beans, pink beans, red beans, purple beans and lavender beans; yellow, tan, green and handsome glossy black; mottled, speckled, dotted and splashed with other color tones. Beans can be round, oval, fat or flat; long and thin; plump and kidney-shaped.

Flavors can range from the robust, hearty or earthy to the delicate and subtle. Shapes can remain firm and neat after cooking, to provide distinctive additions to salads; others can be whirled and smoothed into elegant, velvety purées or creamy soups.

For example, Christmas limas are large brown-mottled beans with a chestnut-like flavor; they can be cooked relatively quickly and be served with style by adding a few drops of olive oil and freshly ground black pepper, or be combined with eggplant, garlic and tomatoes for a superb Provençal casserole with a touch of class. Scarlet runners, with their luscious purple and black coats and potato-like taste, when garnished with a mere hint of butter can be fit for an epicure. Imported red lentils which cook in a jiffy can make a brilliant color statement on a dinner plate to dazzle your guests. And innovative chefs are pairing beans with unexpected and often luxurious partners: garbanzos tossed with imported truffles; white beans and an herbed vegetable mousse; or aromatic green lentils with a simple grilled salmon fillet—if you eat fish. Beans and lentils can be exciting.

Unusual beans can give a fresh appeal to enliven old favorite recipes in your collection. Or familiar varieties of beans, the ones you've always cooked for your family, can be given a new twist with some of the innovative ways and ideas in this guide.

Healthy eating

"Beans once a day keep the doctor away." Legumes are also being widely discussed because the medical world considers them healthful—although nutrition alone never guaranteed popularity. Still, specialists in the field of digestive diseases and cardiac problems not only heartily endorse beans, but suggest they should be eaten daily.

At the same time, of course, legumes (known as pulses in Britain), make wonderful comfort food— inviting, warm, nostalgic "Mom-food" to conjure up childhood memories—a poultice against cold weather. (After all, poultice and pulses come from the same Latin root for porridge meal.) It's hard to beat the tempting aroma and flavor from a bean pot—well-seasoned, slow-simmered, warm and bubbly.

Easy choosing

Where can you find the new beans? They're no longer hard to find: natural-food, health-food and specialty stores usually carry a wide assortment, often in bulk. Local ethnic grocery stores carry good selections, especially those that are featured in their particular cuisine. You can buy them at markets such as The Bean Bag in Oakland, or Phipps Ranch in Pescadero, California, or Dean & DeLuca in New York City. Appendix 2 has full details of addresses for easy buying by phone, FAX or mail. And something else: you can find a surprising number of unusual varieties in seed catalogs, if you are a gardener wanting to grow your own rare-type beans.

Thrifty buying

Another bonus about beans that is worth remembering: they are extremely economical. They are an inexpensive source of protein, compared to meat. They can feed a crowd when you need a potluck dish or the family stays for supper—and they're perfect for holiday entertaining. The dazzling varieties of boutique beans are well worth the cost—between $3 and $5 per pound on average; varieties sold in supermarkets and health food stores are priced at only pennies per serving.

Easy gourmet cooking

Many people have shied away from beans because they think cooking them is time-consuming, but when beans are freshly harvested or bought directly from a bean farm, pre-soaking is often unnecessary or can be minimized for certain varieties. New methods can radically reduce cooking time: armed with a pressure cooker, you can produce tender garbanzos in less than an hour and lentils in only a few minutes. Microwaving canned or leftover cooked beans can bring you meals in a flash. Beans lend themselves to all kinds of preparation, so when you cook a pot of them, cook plenty. Boil up twice as many beans as you need for a recipe, then you'll have a handy batch of prepared beans ready to use at another meal—a salad, soup or casserole. Many bean dishes can be put on hold in the fridge for hours, or even overnight.

Other products

This is just the beginning of the new wave of luscious legumes: already in the markets are ready-to-make mixes of multi-colored beans and seasonings, microwaveable pouches of seasoned, quick-cooking beans, bean flakes and bean pastas such as cellophane noodles and bean threads. And the new fun Bean Chips™ (made of black-eyed beans, corn and rice flour) are easy to find in health-food stores and produce markets, many retail grocery chains, and soon all over the country.

Bean bounty

The following chapters outline the fascinating historical background of beans and peas, and show why they're nutritious. If you're eager to start cooking, though, fast forward to Chapters 5 and 6 for up-to-the-minute tips on bean preparation and tempting recipes using varieties old and new. The cornucopia of recipes is of international scope, inspired by other cultures and other peoples, with plenty of stylish ideas to spark your imagination for cooking with flair, and to make "heirloom" beans part of your own family tradition. Enjoy the bounty, the beauty and the benefits of beans!

1. New Mexican Appaloosa

2. Brown tepary

3. Mung

4. Adzuki

5. Snowcap

6. Christmas lima

7. Steuben yellow-eye

8. Anasazi®

9. Black runner

10. White tepary

11. Swedish brown

12. Scarlet runner

13. Pinkito

14. Navy

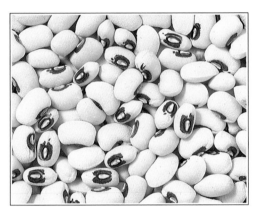

15. Black-eye

16. Pinto

17. Baby lima

18. Garbanzo

19. Great northern

20. Red

21. Cranberry

22. Black

23. Large lima

24. Dark red kidney

CHAPTER 2

Family History

You probably first learned about beans in nursery school when you listened to the tale of Jack and his magic Beanstalk. But the real story of beans, peas and lentils is a romantic one dating back to prehistory.

From a few simple indigenous types growing wild in certain parts of the world, humans have labored and cultivated beans to produce hundreds of forms, shapes, colors and flavors, depending on climate and plant-disease factors, or taste preferences linking them to particular ethnic groups. For thousands of years, people valued the seeds, taking them as prized possessions when they left home: precious sacks of beans were traded in distant markets and loaded on pack animals along ancient caravan routes crossing desert and mountain, or stowed as cargoes in sailing vessels spanning the ocean. African slaves often brought a handful of beans with them to the New World, even if they had nothing else.

The Legume Family

Beans belong to the *Leguminosae* (pod-bearing) family of plants called *legumes* (an interesting word that goes back by way of French to the Latin for "to pick by hand"). This group contains about 13,000 species that produce pods that split open as they mature, releasing the seeds. They have been remarkably adaptable to a wide range of climates if planted at suitable times and so, over the centuries, they have spread to all continents. They will grow almost anywhere in the world where sufficient water is available and where soil can be ploughed. However, edible legumes pre-date the plough.

Prehistoric hunting and gathering tribes were nomadic, subsisting on whatever berries, seeds, insects and other foods they found in fields, woods and desert, such as wild beans, wild peas, wild grains and wild-bee honey. Although many vegetable foods leave no archeological traces, wild forms of beans, lentils and chickpeas have shown up in the Middle East, Central America and parts of Europe. And when ancient peoples settled and began growing crops, legumes were among the earliest plants to be domesticated. Primitive farmers learned to select seeds from the wild plants and to sow those that had high yield and resistance to pests, diseases and climate stress.

Early evidence

So where and when did legumes originate? Probably in Southeast Asia (rather than in the Middle East, as researchers originally thought). The Spirit Cave, situated near the border between Myanmar (Burma) and Thailand, contained fossilized seeds closely resembling modern beans and peas that had been there since about 9750 B.C., according to radiocarbon dating—1,500 years before agriculture began in the Middle East or Central America.

By about 8000 B.C., early forms of chickpeas, fava beans (broad beans) and lentils were being cultivated in the Middle East, in what is known as the Fertile Crescent—a broad arc curving northward and eastward from the Mediterranean coast (now Israel) to the

Zagros Mountains near the border between Iraq and Iran.

In North America, sometime between 7000 B.C. and 5000 B.C., the inhabitants of caves in the Tamaulipas Mountains of Mexico gathered runner beans. In South America, about 6000 B.C., the Incas of Peru, whose diet was mainly vegetarian, were growing beans along with their corn, squash, potatoes, groundnuts and avocados. And in ceremonial graves, they were placing bags of cooked beans beside bodies of young boys sacrificed in Incan rituals—probably as symbolic meals for the dead children's journey to the Other World.

In the ancient world

The Bible has several references to legumes: in Genesis 25:34, Jacob gave Esau bread and pottage of lentils. In Ezekiel 4:9, bread was made of "wheat and barley, and beans and lentils and millet and fitches" (archaic for vetch). And in Daniel 1:12-16, Daniel refused to eat the "unclean" meats of Nebuchadnezzar, the King of Babylon, and chose instead a vegetarian diet of legumes and water—and appeared noticeably healthier after a period of ten days.

In Sumer, where the basic diet was chickpeas, lentils and beans, as well as grains and root vegetables, the people discovered early that the rotation of crops made land more fertile and productive, alternating the growing of wheat or rye with peas, chickpeas, lentils and fava beans. Ancient Greeks made pastes from lentils and beans as well as from grain. To show the importance attached to legumes, four leading families in ancient Roman derived their surnames from the Latin words for the four major legumes known then: Cicero from *Cicer arietinum* (chickpea), Fabius from *Vicia faba* (fava bean), Piso from *Pisum* (pea) and Lentulus from *Lens* (lentil).

In the Middle Ages

Legumes were part of the staple diet in the northern European lands between A.D. 500 and 1450. Bad weather often destroyed many of the grain crops, so coarse breads were made from mixtures of bean, pea and rye flours. Many impoverished people staved off starvation by subsisting on legume porridges. Pottages of puréed beans were standard fare in poorer households, and the medieval cook used dried beans and dried peas at most meals, similar to the way we use potatoes today.

Legumes and religion

Since ancient times, people have believed that rings and circles possessed magical properties. Circular symbolism was carried over to the table, and foods were often thought to have mysterious or special power, to symbolize fertility, prosperity, good luck and immortality. Legumes such as beans, peas and lentils were round and abundant, and were used whenever the mystery of life had to be explained, or when offerings were needed to thank or please the gods or to ward off the demons.

It's surprising how many beliefs originating in ancient times survive to today. In the Jewish kitchen, lentils have always symbolized the cycle of life and are part of days of rejoicing, for births, bar and bat mitzvahs and weddings. The rounded lentil was used to combat the evil influence of Lilith who was feared as a threat to pregnant women and to children. At the Watch Night meal before a bar mitzvah, cooked legumes such as fava beans and chickpeas are eaten, to help the child's lucky star.

On the subcontinent of India, at the *shradha*, a Vedic Indian ritual paying homage to a dead relative, a feast consisting of several courses all containing legumes, is still prepared in its full tradition today.

As a result of Hindu teachings against the killing of animals, using legumes for food in India was and still is unequaled anywhere else in the world.

Now let's focus on the major members in the legume family:

Beans

The world's most important beans are the common kidney bean *(Phaseolus vulgaris)* and lima bean *(P.limensis)*, natives of the Americas, dating back about 8,000 years, the fava bean *(Vicia faba)* (usually called broad bean in Europe), a native of the Middle East, and the soybean *(Glycine)*, native of Asia, cultivated more than 4,000 years ago.

Common beans

Beans of the Americas *(Phaseolus)*—the kind we're most likely to see in supermarkets—were apparently first domesticated from a common wild ancestor about 7,000 years ago in both Mexico and Peru. The tribes in the Tehuacan Valley of Mexico started cultivating small-seeded, light-colored varieties, while at the same time the natives in Callejon de Huaylas, in Peru, were developing large-seeded, dark-colored types. Ancient Peruvians were prodigious farmers, and by the first century A.D. they had harnessed Andean rivers to irrigate lush fields. In fact, they cultivated 40 percent more land then than modern-day Peruvian farmers.

Indians would sow beans and squash among rows of corn so that the legume vines conveniently entwined and climbed the corn stalks for support, thus eliminating the need for weeding between rows. Since Indian trails crisscrossed the American continent, this "Three Sisters" farming practice spread gradually all over

North and South America, as Indian groups explored, migrated, traded or ceremonially exchanged gifts with tribes in other parts. Beans were able to survive in a range of contrasting climates; they were important foods for the Pueblo Indians in the hot, arid Southwest, and also sustained the Indian tribes of cold, damp, Northeast America. By the time the Spanish and Portuguese explorers "discovered" the New World, dozens of varieties were already flourishing, including the lima beans of the Peruvian highlands, Anasazi beans in the arid Southwest, and small white beans of the cold Northern plains.

Tepary beans (*P. acutifolius*) were a staple of the O'odham Indians (Papago and Pima) who lived near present-day Tucson, Arizona. In fact, the Spanish called them "Bean People" because, at one time, the average O'odham ate ³⁄₄ pound of these beans daily! The Papago tribe derived its name from *papáh*, the word for beans in the Papago language.

Indian tribes of America considered beans more than food and made them part of their religious rites: they valued yellow, blue, red, white, pinto and black beans because they symbolized their six cardinal points—North, East, South, West, zenith and nadir.

Stories of beans are interwoven in folk tales, such as a legend of the tepary among the Tohono (Papago) Indians of the O'odham:

> *"The white bean is the child of the Desert People. It is born here and grows here and endures dryness. When it doesn't rain enough, the white bean still comes up. The Desert People will always eat it and live here. The Milky Way is said to be white beans, living clear across the sky. Beans grow in abundance and we see them scattered across the sky."*

By the 15th and 16th centuries, Spanish explorers

found Indians growing beans throughout Latin America. Christopher Columbus probably discovered American beans growing in Huevitas, Cuba. Cabez de Vaca "rediscovered" beans in Florida in 1528, and shortly afterwards Jacques Cartier found them growing at the mouth of the St. Lawrence River. When Samuel de Champlain was among the Eastern Abenaki Indians on Cape Cod in 1605, he described "an abundance of Brazilian beans which they cultivate." In the 17th century, British colonists found bean crops in New England and Virginia, and learned from the American Indians not only the practice of planting beans with rows of corn but also how to make succotash, a casserole mixture of corn and beans.

American beans made no impression in Europe until conquistadores penetrated Mexico in 1519 when the French word for bean, *haricot*, was taken from the Aztec *ayacotl*.

The story goes that in 1528 American beans were sent to Pope Clement VII who gave them to Canon Pietro Valeriano in Florence. Valeriano cultivated them carefully in a pot, approved his first crop and gave some to Alessandro de Medici. Then in 1533, when Alessandro was helping Catherine de Medici to prepare supplies for her journey to France to marry Henry II, he included bags of New World beans. (When royalty traveled in those days, they brought everything with them, because they weren't sure what they would find along the way!)

However, the Europeans were slow to accept the beans, and two centuries were to pass before the French planted them in quantity on lands near Soissons in 1749. The particular variety of beans planted there today is still known in France as *soissons*.

Portuguese and Spanish explorers, traders and empire builders subsequently spread the cultivation of

American bean varieties around the world, so that by the early 17th century they were popular crops in Europe, Africa and Asia. The largest bean producers in the world today are India, Brazil, China and Mexico, but beans are also a major crop in fourteen states in America, particularly Michigan. The community of Fairgrove in Michigan celebrates the annual harvest with a Bean Festival usually held each Labor Day weekend.

Twelve major bean varieties are grown commercially in the United States. California, the second largest producer after Michigan, grows six of them: light red kidneys, dark red kidneys, pinks and small whites, plus large limas and baby limas, most of which are produced in the Central Valley counties of San Joaquin, Stanislaus, Fresno, Kern and Tulare.

The six other commercial varieties not widely grown in California are black beans, cranberry beans, Great Northern beans, navy beans, pinto beans and yellow-eyed beans.

The *Phaseolus vulgaris* common bean has been developed into literally hundreds of varieties, and now the race is on, not only to produce infinite variations of all colors, but to revive the growing of hardy "heirlooms" that early settlers once cultivated and relished.

Lima beans

Another New World bean, *Phaseolus limensis,* originated about 6000 B.C. in the highlands of Peru, taking its name from the capital city of Lima (though in England, the lima bean is still called by its original name of butter bean), and the cultivation of limas was spread throughout the Americas and Caribbean by Indians. Bean farming was extensive in the Andes in pre-Columbian times. In fact, the word "Andes" means "terraces" in Spanish because explorers found the ancient peoples had cut the high slopes into narrow strips for growing crops including beans, watered by intricate canal systems to augment the meager rainfall.

Some say that it was Captain John Harris of the U.S. Navy who brought lima beans back from Peru early in the 19th century, and popularized them in America. However, the Spanish and Portuguese travelers and traders at an earlier time had probably had a hand in introducing them in the United States: they had already shipped them back to Spain and Portugal, and when Iberian fishermen settled with their wives along the New England coast, they were using them in preference to other American beans in their old-country recipes. The slave trade introduced the lima bean to Africa where it is one of the main varieties in the tropical belt.

The city of Tracy in San Joaquin County, California, now prides itself on being "the baby lima bean capital of the world," and celebrates the harvest with a lively annual Bean Festival, usually held in August.

Fava beans

While these beans have an Italian name in the United States, they are often referred to as broad beans in areas of Europe, and for centuries the broad bean was the basic dish of the English peasant-worker.

These Old World beans have been found in Stone Age sites, prehistoric Swiss lake settlements, and in the ruins of Troy, thriving in a range of climates. These beans don't like hot weather but don't mind a freezing, so they have been grown during the winter in warm regions and during the summer in cooler lands. One large-seeded form appears to have originated in the Mediterranean basin, while a small-seeded variety perhaps started in an area extending from the Middle East to west of the Himalayas. Favas have been cultivated from China to England, Iran to Spain, Africa to South America.

Ancient Chaldeans in Babylonia believed that after death they could be reborn as fava beans; Egyptians worshiped beans as a symbol of life and dedicated temples to them. In Homer's Greece, the three principal vegetables were fava beans, lentils and chickpeas—apart from onions and garlic. The Greeks even used beans in their politics: Athenians used them as tokens when counting votes in the election of magistrates, with white beans meaning "for" and the black "against." And about A.D. 100, when the philosopher Plutarch instructed his followers to "abstain from beans," he was telling them to avoid political issues, not advising about diet.

In ancient Rome, when the festival of Saturn was celebrated with feasting and revelry, the master of the Saturnalian revels was chosen by drawing beans, when the man who received a piece of cake containing a fava bean became the king of the festivities (a custom transferred later to Christianity's Twelfth Night tradition). Romans not only used beans extensively in their cuisine, they even gambled with them. And at funeral wakes, the mourners would offer dishes of beans— perhaps to propitiate the gods and ensure immortality.

Although fava beans have been grown and eaten for centuries in the Old World, their popularity waned in Europe when they were gradually supplanted by New World beans. The limas and so-called "French" beans became fashionable after the exploration and settling of the American continents brought cross-Atlantic trading.

Fava beans were introduced into the United States as far back as 1602, but strangely enough, they haven't been a popular item in this country except where immigrants from Mediterranean areas arrived here and raised crops of favas for their own use. But fava beans never lost popularity around the Mediterranean: an important item in the diet of common people of the Ancient Egyptian Empire was a bean cake called *tamia*—which is still eaten today in Egypt and known as *tamiya*. In Cairo, cooks prepare fava beans overnight in copper caldrons then deliver them to restaurants, and in the streets, vendors sell *ful* (boiled beans) or *ful medamas* (baked beans). Algerians eat fava beans as a side dish with couscous; and the mountain people of Algeria prepare *bissar*, which is dried beans cooked in water and oil to make a gruel, eaten hot or cold. In Turkey, the beans are cooked in a piquant sauce called *pilaki* and served cold as appetizers. In Nigeria, boiled fava beans are mashed and combined with coconut milk.

Soybeans

These Oriental beans probably originated in Manchuria, in northern China, and farmers cultivated them as early as 5,000 years ago. In China and the subcontinent of India, the peoples were conquered at various times by hordes of nomadic Tartar and Mongol horsemen from the steppes of Central Asia. Historians speculate that the mostly vegetarian diet of the Chinese evolved because the people hated their invaders (whose diet was mainly meat and dairy products) and wanted to distance themselves from them. But, more likely, the Chinese were forced to eat a predominantly vegetarian diet because of their poverty and a population crowded on a land area reduced by the invaders' occupation. (In addition, the Chinese had difficulty digesting cows' milk; we know now that many people in that part of the world don't have sufficient stomach enzymes to cope with dairy products.)

Consequently they learned over a period of thousands of years to fully utilize the versatile soybean as sprouts, as oil and products such as soy "milk," soy "curd" or soy "cheese." Even in China today, full use is made of the ubiquitous soybean: the center of Chinese village life may well be the soy factory that makes and sells tofu, beancurd, beancurd-sticks and skins, and noodles.

It appears that soybeans originally came to the American continent in 1804, when sailors loaded a Yankee clipper ship bound for the United States using soybeans as an inexpensive ballast—although when they arrived in the United States, they didn't eat the beans. They dumped them to make room for cargo. The first use of soybeans in America was in soaps, paints and varnish.

American farmers first grew soybeans in 1829, raising a variety for soy sauce, then during the Civil War thirty years later, soldiers used soybeans as "coffee berries" to make a synthetic brew when real coffee was scarce. Nobody thought of eating them whole, fresh or dried.

In the late 1800s, a number of farmers began to raise soybeans as a forage for cattle; then in 1904, George Washington Carver at the Tuskeegee Institute in Alabama discovered that soybeans provided valuable protein and oil.

But soybeans caught on in a big way in the United States only about thirty years ago, and now American farmers grow almost as many crops of soybeans as they do wheat. You may not realize how much you make use of soy today. These beans, their oils and other products are put in an array of foods such as margarines, mayonnaise, shortenings, cooking oils and filled milks, as well as in soaps, detergents, paints and plastics.

Peas

Garden peas

This pea *(Pisum sativum)* may have originated in India, as the word is believed to be from the Sanskrit language, although historians usually place its early beginnings in lands ranging from the Middle East into Central Asia. In fact, the place of origin is obscure because the pea's original ancestor is now extinct. Peas carbon-dated at 9750 B.C. have been found at archeological sites in Southeast Asia, and dated back to 6750 B.C. at Qalat Jarmo in northeastern Iraq.

Since peas flourish in cool climates, they probably traveled along the more northern trade routes from Asia to Europe, through Mesopotamia, Sumer, Assyria and Phoenicia. Both the Greeks and the Romans enjoyed peas year-round, fresh as well as dried, so that Trajan's market sold some thirty-seven varieties of peas at one season or another. They were grown in Mycenae, and in Pericles' time the street vendors of Athens sold hot pea soup.

In the Middle Ages, about A.D. 800, King Charlemagne commanded that peas be planted throughout his realm:

> *"Pease porridge hot, pease porridge cold.*
> *Pease porridge in the pot, nine days old."*

Pottages or porridges made from dried peas were given to the poor, and eaten by everyone as a Lenten or fast-day dish. Ubiquitous pease pudding was probably the medieval equivalent of today's French fries.

But in reverse chic, peas became fashionable as a

novelty in high court circles, and were considered a "royal dish" in 1533 when Catherine de Medici brought her *piselli novelli* from Florence on her marriage to Henry II of France.

In the 1800s, the Austrian monk, Gregor Mendel, used peas in his experiments on genetics.

The first peas in the New World may have been those brought to Isabella Island in 1493 by Christopher Columbus, although there seems to be some confusion about mention of peas in America because early explorers may have confused them with the cultivation of beans. Historical journals mention Spaniards finding peas growing in New Mexico in 1540. According to Jacques Cartier, the Hochelagan Indians in 1535 were raising peas where Montreal now stands and French traders had discovered Indians growing peas along the Ottawa River in 1613. Captain Bartholomew Gosnold first planted peas in New England in 1602 on the island of Cuttyhunk. In 1608 Captain John Smith wrote of feasting on "Virginia pease," and in 1614 of Indians growing them in New England. Settlers were growing peas in the governor's garden at Plymouth by 1629. General John Sullivan destroyed peas and other crops in 1779, during a raid against Iroquois Indians of western New York State.

Black-eyed peas

This favorite of the Southern states of America is not really a pea but a relative of the mung bean and needs a slightly warmer climate than the regular pea.

Although many people associate this pea with Afro-Americans and believe that it had its origins in Africa, the black-eye probably grew wild in China and came with travelers along the Silk Route to the Middle East, to Arabia, East Africa, and across to West Africa. From there, black-eyed peas (and others in the cowpea family) were transported in the holds of slave ships to the Caribbean islands and thence to the U.S. Southern states. Although black-eyes are still grown in the South, quantities are produced in California and shipped around the globe including Africa and the Far East—thus, in a way, completing the circle.

Chickpeas (garbanzos)

The large round yellow chickpea grows in a pod and so belongs in the Leguminosae family; however it's not really a pea but a member of a subfamily that needs a warm climate.

Because humans have been cultivating it for so long, the original wild ancestor of the chickpea no longer exists. Although they were supposedly native to the region south of the Caucasus and north of Persia, remains in pre-Neolithic Sicily and Neolithic Switzerland suggest that chickpeas were probably a food of those times. They were known to have been in the Hanging Gardens of Babylon, and common in ancient Egypt. Chickpeas and bacon were placed in amphorae in Pompeii and dispatched to other regions of the Roman Empire around the Mediterranean. Some historians have speculated that Cicero had derived his name from a wart on his nose that grew to the size of a chickpea (*cicer*, in Latin). However, Cicero was not a nickname; it had been his family name for many generations when these legumes were a valuable staple of the diet.

The chickpea became especially popular in Spain because it reached there through two cultural routes: first with the Roman legions and later the Moorish conquerors from North Africa. The Spanish, in turn, took the chickpea to the New World and their other colonies around the globe—Columbus himself carried chickpea seeds to the Caribbean.

In the Jewish kitchen, chickpeas are a traditional vegetable: North African Jews include them in couscous eaten at noon after the morning service of Rosh Hashanah; Eastern European Jews also eat chickpeas at Rosh Hashanah, but prefer them plain, simply sprinkled with salt and pepper. Typical foods at the Purim feast are chickpeas along with *kreplach* (filled noodle dough), *sambusak* (stuffed pastries), and turkey. *Falafel* (chickpea patties) and *hummus* (chickpea dip) have come to typify Israeli cuisine; they are sold by street vendors in Israel and are popular for Yom Ha'atzma'ut (Israeli Independence Day) on April 19.

Lentils

Part of the human diet for over 8,000 years, lentils were among the first vegetables to be cultivated when nomadic tribes settled and took up farming. Their origin seems to have been northeastern Iraq at Qalat Jarmo where seed remains have been carbon-dated to about 6750 B.C. and at Halicarnassus in Turkey to about 5500 B.C. In Anatolia, ancient vessels containing lentils bear markings that identify them as having been grown in Sumer. Lentils found in Egypt date back to 3000 B.C. Remains of a lentil purée were discovered in a Twelfth Dynasty tomb at Thebes. And in 800 B.C., lentils were being grown in the Babylonian gardens of King Merodach-Baladan. The cultivation of lentils spread from the Greeks and up the valley of the River Danube to the Balkans, reaching southern Germany by Neolithic times.

Early on, the process of drying lentils to preserve them was discovered, so that by Grecian times lentils were eaten in and out of season. When Athens was at the height of its glory, Ancient Greeks of all classes ate lentils as a diet staple. Some of their distinguished philosophers ate them ostentatiously to demonstrate they were above self-indulgence and worldly pleasures; Hippocrates prescribed them for liver ailments.

In ancient Rome, where it was common to borrow or assume the lifestyles or habits of the Greeks, lentils became part of the diet, approved by Virgil and Pliny, and included in a cookbook by Apicius. The Roman Emperor Heliogabalus at one of his spectacular banquets offered his guests a dish of lentils mixed with topazes. Since Romans were especially partial to the small red Egyptian lentils, a steady stream of merchant vessels brought them from Alexandria to Ostia. And when an obelisk was shipped to Rome to stand in front of St. Peter's, nearly three million Roman pounds of lentils were crammed beneath this vessel's special cargo.

During the Middle Ages, many peasants subsisted on boiled lentils or peas with black bread and oatmeal. About A.D. 800, King Charlemagne ordered lentils planted throughout his lands, and in the 16th century the French physician Ambroise Paré recommended lentils against smallpox. Lentils were made fashionable at the French court: the tiny green lentils of France (then and now considered some of the best) were referred to as *lentilles à la reine*. The Queen was Marie, wife of Louis XV, and the lentil dish was named in honor of the vegetable highly prized in her native Poland.

Lentils reached India in very early times and the area now grows fifty varieties, so it's not surprising that the subcontinent is the greatest consumer of lentils in the world. One Parsee dish called *dahnsak* instructs cooks to use a blend of three to nine kinds of lentils.

Lentils may have first arrived in America when Father St. John of the Jesuit missionaries brought the legumes to the Iroquois Indians along the St. Lawrence River.

Today, however, the best growing conditions for lentils are considered to be in the Pacific Northwest in a region called "The Palouse" of eastern Washington and northern Idaho.

CHAPTER 3

Bravo for Beans!

We'd all like to live the fantasy of having foods that look, smell and taste good proving to be the most nutritious. With a savory dish of beans or peas, it turns out to be true. Beans are packed with goodness. Bite for bite, any way you eat them, dried beans are high-powered building blocks for good nutrition. (Although immature fresh beans are delicious, they don't have quite the same nutritional values as legumes allowed to mature in the pod and dry.) Beans have always been a favorite for terrific flavor and economy, but today they are acknowledged to be a near-perfect food by many health-related groups, such as the American Heart Association, the American Cancer Society, and the American Diabetes Association.

So what's in it for you? The nutritional values of the many varieties, including new ones and "heirlooms," are very similar. Here's how they weigh up:

High in dietary fiber	*Low in fat*
High in complex carbohydrates	*Low in sodium*
High in protein	*No cholesterol*

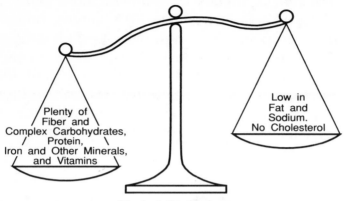

Fig. 1. A Good Balance

That's a *good* balance—those highs and lows are all great! Eating "what's good for you" is often equated with hard-to-swallow, boring or unpleasant foods—but now with the many new varieties of dried beans, good eating can be fun and delicious.

What's in a Bean?

Plenty of complex carbohydrates and fiber

Dried beans and peas are loaded with complex carbohydrates (starches and fiber)—a natural healthy source of energy just right for today's active lifestyle. Recent U.S. dietary guidelines tell us that as we cut back on fat, carbohydrates should account for more of our daily calories. But aren't carbohydrates fattening? No, they're no more fattening than any other food and, in fact, ounce for ounce, they provide half the calories of fat. Foods such as legumes, whole-grain breads and cereals and veggies provide complex (high-fiber) carbohydrates that your body digests and absorbs more slowly than simple (low-fiber) carbs. such as table sugar, candy, cakes and pastries, so legumes satisfy hunger for longer periods of time. In 3½ ounces of cooked Anasazi beans, you'll get about 21 grams of carbohydrate. No official dietary recommendations have yet been set for fiber as they have for vitamins, minerals and other nutrients, but one-half cup of delicious cooked navy beans contains a whopping 6.8 grams of total fiber (about twenty-five percent of the daily fiber intake suggested by the National Cancer Institute) whereas a one-third cup of dry oat bran has only 4.0 grams of total fiber. See Figure 2 for a comparison of fibrous foods.

Fig. 2. Fiber Content of Some Common Foods

Food Group	Total dietary fiber (gm)	Soluble fiber (gm)
Legumes:		
Navy beans, dried, cooked, ½ cup	6.78	2.29
Pinto beans, dried, cooked, ½ cup	5.90	1.84
Kidney beans, canned, ½ cup	5.75	1.45
White beans: dried, cooked, ½ cup	5.07	1.48
canned, ½ cup	4.98	1.50
Pinto beans, canned, ½ cup	4.34	1.01
Pork and beans, canned, ½ cup	3.74	1.84
Black-eyed peas, canned, ½ cup	3.21	0.35
Lima beans, canned, ½ cup	3.02	0.79
Garbanzo beans, canned, ⅓ cup	2.08	0.32
Cereals:		
Oat bran, ⅓ cup	4.03	2.01
Whole-wheat flour, 2½ tablespoons	2.80	0.35
Whole-wheat bread, 1 slice	1.53	0.34
Fruits:		
Apple, 1 small	2.76	0.97
Banana, 1 small	2.18	0.64
Grapefruit, ½ medium	1.46	0.90

(Source: Adapted from James W. Anderson, M.D. and Susan R. Bridges, B.A.: "Dietary Fiber Content of Selected Foods." *American Journal of Clinical Nutrition,* Vol. 47, pp. 440-7, 1988)

Fiber—the parts of fruits, vegetables and grains that can't be broken down by digestion—is found in every plant food we eat: whole grains and cereals, fruits and vegetables, nuts, seeds and especially beans, peas and lentils. After digestive enzymes have extracted nutrients from food, the indigestible residue is fiber whose job is to give you the bulk that promotes regularity in the digestive tract. Fiber's major service to your body is to keep digestion ticking along in orderly fashion.

There are two main types of fiber: soluble and insoluble. *Insoluble* fiber, which can't hold onto water particles, is the cellulose, lignin and hemicellulose—the "woody" part of husks and shells we think of as "roughage" that moves quickly through the digestive system. It's found in dried legumes, wheat bran, whole grains, fruits such as dried figs, and in vegetables. *Soluble* fiber is the pectins, mucilages and gums (especially guar gum), found in the cell walls of dried legumes, oats and barley, apples, pears and citrus fruits. It dissolves in water during digestion, and forms a gel-like substance which helps the body handle fats, cholesterol and carbohydrates.

Each type of fiber has its own merits and function in the body. You don't want to focus on one or the other because you need both for good health. The great point about beans is that they have rich portions of both.

How much fiber should you have? Unfortunately, Americans consume only 10 to 20 grams of fiber daily—whereas some African tribes eat up to six times that amount in meals that usually include a fair quantity of beans. Rural Africans, for instance, who consume up to 150 grams of fiber a day, are less likely to have diverticulitis (formation and inflammation of pouches in the colon), appendicitis, gallstones, hemorrhoids, varicose veins, diabetes and some forms of coronary heart disease. But you wouldn't want that much fiber, and shouldn't need it. In fact, the American Dietetic Association discourages anything over 50 grams daily, as a safeguard against food passing through too quickly, resulting in poor mineral and vitamin absorption. Medical authorities suggest as a practical goal that adult Americans should gradually double their fiber intake to 30 or 40 grams a day. So what good will that do?

* Fiber makes stool easier to pass, so it corrects constipation as well as problems linked to straining—diverticular pouches in the colon, hemorrhoids and varicose veins.

* Fiber acts like a kitchen broom, sweeping the intestines and colon clean of cancer-causing wastes, and swishing stools through the digestive tract.

* Fiber may help ward off pancreatic cancer, and help protect against cancers of the breast and prostate.

* Fiber-rich diets have been shown to lower total blood cholesterol as much as 19 percent in patients whose diets included two cups of beans a day. Not only that: fiber can raise the proportion of desirable HDL (high-density lipoprotein) in the bloodstream, to protect against heart disease. Fiber diminishes the amount of cholesterol the body absorbs from food, and may even alter the amount of cholesterol formed in the liver.

* Fiber may help check the level of fats (triglycerides) in the blood.

* Some studies show that fiber can help lower blood pressure.

* A generous intake of soluble fiber can help reduce

blood-sugar levels, and may decrease the body's need for daily insulin in people with Type I diabetes. For those with Type II diabetes, an increase in soluble fiber may help control diabetes by diet/lifestyle changes alone, without the need for medication—although the debate still continues on this point.

* Fiber is helpful in weight control. Because it cannot be absorbed into your system, fiber gives you almost no calories. For a given number of calories, high-fiber foods give you more to swallow than low-fiber foods.

Some grains and cereals have had their fiber stripped away by the milling and refining process before they reach supermarkets. Fortunately beans—whether dried, canned or frozen—have lost none of their valuable fiber. The only processing is the chewing done by your teeth before the bean fiber enters your stomach. Chewing beans gives your stomach more time to feel full and satisfied, so that a meal appears to be more substantial. The chewing action adds saliva to the beans, and they absorb more liquid as they pass through the intestines—and these additions contribute even more bulk.

One last word on fiber: try to drink eight glasses of water a day, as fiber draws it into your system. Sufficient fluids are important for keeping everything functioning right. Too much fiber with too little liquid can actually cause constipation and blockage.

Plenty of protein

Protein is an essential part of a healthy diet—necessary for such things as sound bone, muscle, cartilage, blood, skin and proper working of lymph glands. A constant supply of protein keeps your body at peak efficiency;

with inadequate protein, you may feel weak and tired, and have a reduced resistance to infection.

Are you getting enough protein from vegetarian meals? When you eat legumes, they are in fact especially versatile protein sources, and low-fat too. You may not realize how much protein comes with eating a wide variety of legumes, grains and vegetables: all dried beans and peas can supply healthy amounts in everyone's diet. One cup of cooked dried lentils or beans, for instance, provides about 25 percent of the daily protein you need. (*Young* fresh beans and peas, however, are less rich in protein because they aren't mature seeds.) Check Figure 3.

So how much do you need? If protein comes from *plant* sources, the U.S. Recommended Daily Allowance (RDA) is 65 grams ($2^{1}/_{3}$ ounces); if protein comes from *animal* sources (meat, fish, poultry, eggs and dairy products), the U.S. RDA is 45 grams ($1^{1}/_{2}$ ounces).

Proteins are made up of amino acids, and your body needs twenty-two different amino acids to function properly. The body itself makes thirteen, so the food you eat must supply the other nine: tryptophan, methionine, lysine, isoleucine, threonine, leucine, histidine, valine and phenylalanine.

Most plant foods are "incomplete" protein. That is, they don't have all nine of those essential amino acids in the right amounts. But you will get more usable protein from legumes, grains and vegetables by combining different plant groups in the same meal (or by adding a dairy product or a little meat), so that they complement each other. Many dietitians recommend a ratio of 60 percent grains/seeds with 35 percent legumes, and 5 percent dark-green leafy vegetables—not necessarily bite for bite, but eaten together at the same meal. In this way, they become smart partners: the incomplete proteins come together in the

Fig. 3. A Vegetarian Guide to Protein*

Food Group	Serving	Protein (gm)
Legumes:		
Black-eyed peas, cooked	1 cup	13
Gt. Northern beans, cooked	1 cup	14
Lentils, cooked	1 cup	16
Lima beans, cooked	1 cup	13
Peanut butter	2 tablespoons	8
Soybean curd (tofu)	2½-inch square	9
Split peas, cooked	1 cup	16
Grains:		
Bran cereal	1 cup	8
Bread, whole-wheat	1 slice	3
Buckwheat pancakes (made with egg and milk)	3 4-inch pancakes	5
Cornbread	2½-inch squares	6
Oatmeal, cooked	1 cup	5
Rice, brown, cooked	1 cup	5
Shredded Wheat cereal	2 biscuits	5
Nuts/seeds:		
Almonds, shelled	1 oz	5
Sesame seeds	1 tablespoon	2
Sunflower seeds	1 tablespoon	2
Walnuts, shelled	1 oz	4
Vegetables:		
Broccoli, cooked	1 cup	5
Collard greens, cooked	1 cup	7
Potato: baked	1 medium	4
scalloped w/cheese	1 cup	13
Spinach, cooked	1 cup	5
Succotash (lima beans & corn), cooked	1 cup	7
Dairy:		
Buttermilk	1 cup	8
Cheese: American	1 oz slice	6
Cheddar	1 oz	7
cottage, low-fat	½ cup	14
Egg, whole	1	6
Milk, skim	1 cup	9
Yogurt, low-fat	1 cup	8

* Except for the Dairy group, protein is "incomplete." See Figure 4 for combining food groups to make proteins "complete."

(Source: *Nutritive Value of American Foods*, Agriculture Handbook No. 456, USDA Agricultural Research Service, Washington, D.C.)

digestive system and your body treats them as "complete." See Figure 4.

Fig. 4. Smart Partners for Protein

How to achieve "complete" protein by combining several different vegetable proteins. The strengths of amino acids in one group can balance the shortcomings in another.

Food Group		Lysine	Isoleucine	Tryptophan	Methionine	Cystine *
				Some essential amino acids		
Legumes:	Beans, black-eyed peas, chickpeas, lentils, peanuts peas, soybeans and tofu	●	●	O	O	O
Grains:	Barley, buckwheat, bulgar, corn, millet, oats, rice, rye, triticale, wheat	O	O	● #	●	●
Seeds:	Pumpkin, sesame, squash, sunflower	O	O #	●	●	●
Nuts:	Almonds, brazils, cashews, coconut, filberts, macadamias, pecans, pine nuts, pistachios, walnuts	O	O	●	●	●
Dairy:	Buttermilk, cheese, eggs, milk, yogurt	●	●	●	●	●

Key: ● = well-supplied with this amino acid
      O = poorly-supplied with this amino acid

Note: * Cystine is not an essential amino acid, but its presence in foods spares methionine, which is essential

      # Except pumpkin seeds and cashew nuts

So you can see that legumes are a great source of usable complete protein when you eat them in combination with other foods; for instance:

Legumes + grain cereals:

Lentil soup with cornbread
Bean and barley soup
Bean and pasta salad
Bean burrito with a wheat tortilla

Legumes + seeds:

Split pea soup with sesame crackers

Legumes + dairy products:

Bean soup with a cheese topping
Bean casserole with a glass of milk
Pizza with a cheese & bean topping

*Legumes + small amounts of meat or meat substitutes
for flavoring.*

The amazing thing is that primitive peoples, rambling and foraging for healthy survival, have been pairing food proteins for centuries if not thousands of years without the chemical knowledge we have today—and without dietitians telling them what to eat! Mexicans have been eating beans and corn; Indians, lentils and rice; Middle Easterners, *hummus* with mashed chickpeas and ground sesame seeds; and early Europeans, pease pottage with coarse wheat breads.

If protein is essential, do you harm your body by giving it *more* than it needs? The answer is yes. Too much protein can have its drawbacks. Your body can't store protein. After you have consumed your caloric needs for the day, excess protein is converted to fat. If this fat isn't burned off as fuel, it becomes part of your body fat—adding pounds, making your kidneys work harder, and maybe triggering certain kinds of cancer.

It's a popular myth that you need extra protein for strenuous exercise. The fact is, a normal diet should supply enough protein for both very active and inactive people. And another myth: high-protein weight-loss diets are best. In fact, Government authorities have declared that high-protein/low-carbohydrate diets are dangerous.

Plenty of iron

Iron is part of the mechanism in blood which supplies oxygen to body cells, for building red blood cells which carry oxygen from the lungs to body cells, and it's a constituent of many digestive enzymes.

Although as a vegetarian you may worry about not getting sufficient daily protein, it's just as important to watch your intake of iron (especially if you're a woman). The good news is that beans contain more iron than such highly touted sources as spinach, other green-leafy vegetables and eggs. (Although foods from animal sources supply larger amounts of iron than beans, they can be loaded with fat and cholesterol.)

One cup of cooked kidney beans supplies a man with almost half the daily amount of iron he needs; and gives a woman about one fourth the amount she should have daily.

Only a fraction of the iron you eat is absorbed, so meals have to contain a lot more of this mineral than your body can use. *Some* iron can be stored in the liver, bone marrow, spleen and other organs, but if you chronically shortchange yourself, these stores are used up eventually. You may be consuming insufficient iron if you're a strict vegetarian confining yourself to only plant foods, or if you are on a drastic low-calorie diet, or if you're a fast-food freak eating mostly junk foods that are nutrient-poor but high in fat, sugar and calories.

Although iron from animal foods is absorbed better than that from plant foods, if you eat a vitamin C-rich vegetable or fruit with the iron-containing food, you'll increase iron absorption. The easy way is just to include a green bell pepper, for instance, or a green chili pepper in the pot of bean chili, or toss in tomatoes at the last minute (otherwise their acid will toughen the beans), or drink some orange juice with the meal. (Make a note, though, that if you have eggs or tea at the same meal, you can block the absorption of much of the iron available in the beans.)

With insufficient iron, you feel weak, fatigued, out of breath, suffer headaches and look pale—a condition called iron-deficient anemia, the most common nutritional deficiency among Americans.

If you suspect you might be anemic and decide to take iron supplements, check first with your doctor about dosage because chronic overdosing can build up to toxic levels. The body has no way to release large amounts of excess iron, and you could damage the liver, pancreas or heart.

Other minerals

Beans contain *phosphorus* and *calcium*, both of which are needed for building and maintaining strong bones and sound teeth, and for regulating processes. Phosphorus is also needed for enzymes used in energy metabolism and for regulating the acid balance in the body. It's not common to have a dietary shortage of phosphorus, but if, for instance, you constantly gulp down antacids you can cause a deficiency. The 416 mg of phosphorus in a one-cup serving of cooked beans supplies about one-third of your normal daily need.

Zinc is needed for normal growth and development: the repair of body tissue, the healing of wounds, and for digestive enzymes and insulin. Insufficient zinc has been linked to dwarfism and iron-deficient anemia. The 1.5 mg of zinc in one cup of cooked red kidney beans supplies about 10 percent of your regular daily need.

Potassium is needed for healthy nerves, muscle contraction, enzyme reactions, protein metabolism, and for maintaining fluid balance in your body. Potassium is especially important if you are an athlete or heavy laborer working hard in the heat, or if you take diuretic medication, or have prolonged diarrhea. The 653 mg of potassium in a one-cup serving of beans provides 14 percent of your daily requirement.

Beans also contain *magnesium,* which you need for building protein, muscle contraction and nerve-impulse transmission. Inadequate magnesium can contribute to high blood pressure, and may lead to seizures and possibly cardiac arrest. Deficiency may result if you have prolonged diarrhea, kidney disease, diabetes, epilepsy, alcoholism, or if you take diuretic medication. The 95 mg of magnesium in a one-cup serving of beans provides about one-fourth of your normal daily needs.

Beans also contain micronutrients or trace minerals, including *copper, manganese, boron* and *iodine.* Boron may help in maintaining mental alertness.

Plenty of vitamins

Beans are among the richest natural sources of the B-complex vitamins—thiamin, pyridoxine, niacin and folic acid. These vitamins trigger the processes that release energy from carbohydrate foods, help absorb and metabolize proteins, help in the formation of red blood cells, and keep your digestive and nervous systems healthy. A one-cup serving of kidney beans meets your folic acid quota and gives you .33 mg of thiamin, which is about one-fourth of your daily needs.

If you are a vegan, you need to pay close attention to vitamin sources. Cooked dried beans and other legumes can play a large role in your diet, along with fortified nutritional yeast, dark-green leafy vegetables, blackstrap molasses and vitamin-fortified margarines.

Low in fat and sodium, and no cholesterol

Most beans and peas have negligible amounts of fat (8 to 10 fat calories per cooked cup out of an average of 212 total calories), so they are naturally good in a low-fat diet. The small amount of fat in beans (less than 2 percent, except for soybeans which have about 5 percent) is polyunsaturated, which means it doesn't have the ability to raise blood cholesterol. And because legumes are plant foods, they of course don't contain dietary cholesterol (unless you use a recipe that adds dairy products or meat).

"Superbean"—Super Prevention

Of course, a diet-change *alone* may not prevent, control or relieve disease. If you already have medical problems, you need to consult your doctor first. Eating a ton of beans won't bring about a cure. Nevertheless, beans are today's perfect health food; they can be a prescription for good nutrition, and the gourmet's ally against a range of maladies found in any doctor's office:

* constipation, and the related problems of hiatus hernia, hemorrhoids, anal fissures and varicose veins

* appendicitis

* cancers of the digestive system and their polyp precursors

* cardiovascular diseases

* diabetes

* intestinal disorders, such as diverticulosis and spastic colon

* gallstones

✳ weight control

✳ food allergies

But because beans are good medicine, don't let this turn you off. It's smart to know that such a delicious and versatile food can be helpful in maintaining good health, and keep you in good shape. Don't think about how healthy beans are—just enjoy them!

Constipation

There are many common misconceptions and false beliefs concerning "proper" bowel habits and what constitutes constipation. The word "regularity" has been in our vocabulary for over 200 years as a genteel way to refer to timely bowel movements, but how regular is regular? Most people experience an occasional brief bout of constipation, an interruption of routine that is minor and temporary, which corrects itself with diet and time. However, chronic constipation can have many different causes, the most common of which are: lack of fiber in the diet, insufficient liquids, lack of exercise, overdoing laxatives, being pregnant, travel, hormonal fluctuations, nerve damage, gynecological surgery such as hysterectomy, or taking medications such as antacids, antidepressant drugs, tranquilizers, anticonvulsants for epilepsy, calcium supplements and iron supplements.

Constipation can lead to a cluster of other complications such as hiatal hernia linked with straining, problems with hemorrhoids, anal fissures and bleeding, and even varicose veins.

Millions of dollars are spent every year on laxatives, many of which are unnecessary and some are even harmful.

Without using harsh chemicals from the drugstore,

you can overcome many of these painful problems simply and naturally (and less expensively) with a well-balanced diet: an increased amount of fibrous foods including all kinds of cooked dried legumes, whole-grain breads and cereals, cooked dried prunes and figs, seed-filled berries, unpeeled fruits, and green-leafy vegetables. Beans are a natural way to "regularity," along with drinking more liquids and taking more exercise.

Appendicitis

An appendectomy is said to be the most frequent emergency operation performed in the United States. The appendix becomes inflamed or infected when the opening between the cecum and the appendix is blocked, a condition that is encouraged by a low-fiber diet or a diet too high in animal fats and proteins. Low-fiber foods produce smaller, harder stools. Pieces of stool called *fecaliths* (literally stones made of feces) can obstruct the opening of the appendix. You could greatly reduce your risk of having this disease by eating more fibrous foods such as beans and other legumes.

Cancers of the digestive system and their polyp precursors

People who live in underdeveloped countries whose diets are high in fiber such as beans, have a much lower incidence of colon cancer than Americans or Europeans eating a low-fiber diet.

When food moves more quickly through the colon, there is less time for toxins and cancer-causing substances to make contact with the bowel lining, and less risk of developing intestinal polyps, or abnormal growths in the mucus surface of the colon, which are believed to be precursors of colon and rectal cancers.

The insoluble fiber in beans speeds the transit of any carcinogens that might be in food, so toxins have a shorter period in which to damage intestinal walls. The soluble fiber helps to bind cancer-causing toxins, making them inactive or preventing them from entering the blood stream.

It just makes good sense to have a wholesome, balanced diet that is low in fat, meatless or moderate in meat, but containing plenty of fibrous foods such as cooked dried beans and peas, fresh unpeeled fruits, fresh vegetables and whole-grain cereals.

Cardiovascular diseases

The good things in beans can be just what the doctor orders: a low-fat, low-sodium diet and a reduced intake of cholesterol. With so many dried legumes to choose from, they can add a wonderful variety to meals, and because they taste good, they can help you stick with a diet designed to reduce risk of heart disease. You can't expect beans to give you complete protection against heart and circulatory problems, because other factors come into play such as genes, heredity, smoking, environment, obesity, stress, and overdosing on animal fats, refined sugar and eggs. While there's no guarantee that foods low in sodium, saturated fats and cholesterol will protect you against clogged arteries, they can tilt the odds in your favor.

Most beans (except soybeans), peas and lentils are naturally low in fats, and have no dietary cholesterol. The tiny amounts of fats in legumes are polyunsaturated, and not the saturated fats that tend to raise serum cholesterol and clog arteries. Recent research has shown that beans even have a substance that helps fight plaque deposits in arteries and can be helpful in reducing risk of blood clots; the guar gum and pectins found in beans can significantly lower serum cholesterol by several notches on your doctor's scale. Bean fiber may reduce cholesterol because beans can increase the excretion of bile acids (which are manufactured from cholesterol) and because the fiber actually binds to cholesterol and whisks it out of your body.

Fiber may also help control the level of triglycerides (fats) in the blood. If you have a diet high in carbohydrates, triglyceride levels generally increase. But when you eat the carbohydrates with plant fiber (and beans are naturally packaged this way) the rise doesn't occur. Fiber in beans may even help lower blood pressure.

Diabetes

Diabetic patients have an increased risk of coronary and circulatory problems, so they will want to take note of the above points. In addition, research studies indicate that generous amounts of soluble fiber can reduce levels of blood sugar and decrease the need for insulin. Beans have the potential to help control diabetes overall.

If you have Type II diabetes, talk with your doctor about gradually stepping up the fiber in your diet, because the effect of soluble fiber might help make the difference between controlling diabetes by diet/lifestyle changes only or with medication. You might be able to get along without insulin or other antidiabetic medicines. The pectins and guar gum in legumes are most effective fibers.

Intestinal disorders

In countries where the people eat less meat and more vegetables (that is, high-fiber foods), they tend to suffer fewer disorders of the colon and rectum. Research at Oxford University, England, has shown that diverticular disease (outpouchings or pockets in the large intestine) is only a third as common among vegetarians as nonvegetarians. Doctors generally encourage patients with diverticulosis to increase their fiber intake at mealtime, instead of the formerly prescribed low-fiber diet "to reduce irritation." Legumes can be a significant part of a doctor's program.

Recent studies on the benefits of fiber are also changing doctors' views about treating spastic colon (irritable bowel syndrome), with fiber regulating the symptoms and muscular activity of the colon. However, first check with your doctor before starting a high-fiber diet, because if you already have a bowel disorder such as an obstruction or severe inflammation, an increase in fiber could make matters worse.

Gallstones

About 10 percent of the American population has gallstones, and each year over half a million Americans have their gallbladders removed because of stones. They are more common in women who have had several pregnancies, overweight people, and people of Scandinavian or Native American descent.

The gallbladder, a pear-shaped sac in the upper right of the abdomen beneath the liver, is a reservoir for bile, a substance produced by the liver which breaks down dietary fats. Normally when fatty foods are digested, the gallbladder expels the bile through a duct into the small intestine. But sometimes this mechanism becomes disordered: the gallbladder may produce too much pigment, or levels of cholesterol and bile acid get out of balance, so bile crystallizes around irritating particles, much the way a pearl forms in an oyster. Gallstones composed mostly of cholesterol (and sometimes calcium) are the result.

Prevention is the best defense: reduce fats and cholesterol in foods, increase dietary fiber, and maintain a sensible weight in relation to your height and frame, without wild swings up and down the bathroom scale. By introducing beans, peas and lentils into your diet, you have one of the best preventives.

Weight control

Quick-weight-loss plans are a big delusion: the diets themselves fail to succeed and the health effects can be disastrous. If you are interested in slimming down (and who isn't in America?), but don't want to give up favorite foods and flavors, here's a tip: reduce the portions of all your meals and add a daily serving of cooked dried beans, peas or lentils. Those lovely legumes and other fibrous foods will help regulate your body weight. You won't think you're "on a diet."

The fiber and complex carbohydrates will reward you with the satisfaction of chewing, a quick transit time through your digestive system and a balancing of fats and sugars in your blood stream. The beans will give you a full, satisfied feeling in your tummy, and send messages to your brain that you have eaten sufficient food. You won't feel deprived. You don't have to give up favorite foods—just eat them in smaller amounts and let them play a minor role. Choose recipes that feature beans in greater proportion to any other ingredient. Adding cooked beans to a dish swings the balance in favor of low-calorie ingredients. By regularly eating beans and changing calorie/fiber ratios, you will be altering the proportions at mealtimes, until you are changing your body's proportions—gradually. We're not talking about rapid weight loss (which generally rebounds in a "yo-yo" effect), but you won't notice you're dieting as you slim down to normal. And with all the new varieties of beans waiting for you to try out and toss into recipes, meals can still be delicious and interesting, with great eye-appeal and taste pleasure.

Rearrange your refrigerator and pantry by storing high-calorie items at the back of the shelves in opaque containers. Bring glass jars of beans to the forefront: the beautiful, brilliant colors and shapes will give you inspiration and help get you motivated to this new approach to foods.

Food allergies

Allergies to all kinds of foods are common, and millions of sensitive people not only may have to avoid foods they like, but suffer nutritional deficiencies because of poorly balanced meals. The good news is that beans have been classified by the U.S. Department of Health and Human Services as one of the least allergenic foods. Allergic reactions are rarely linked to eating legumes, because they are usually preservative-free. Dried beans don't need much processing or the addition of unwanted preservatives before they reach your kitchen. Many people are sensitive to additives such as flavorings, colorings and spices, but these are generally not used with fresh or dried beans, peas and lentils.

However, canned or frozen packages of beans and other commercially produced bean products might contain chemical preservatives that you want to avoid, so it's best to read ingredients labels. Most food producers spell out all ingredients on cans or boxes, but if information is incomplete and you are unsure, write to the food manufacturers, change brands or don't buy the product.

Calcium disodium EDTA is added to some canned beans to help them retain color and firmness. In some cases, you can throw out the offending additive by thoroughly draining and rinsing the beans. But beans canned without this additive are available, and they still have acceptable color and firmness.

So problems with legumes are few. In the next chapter we'll discuss a few drawbacks and how to cope with them.

CHAPTER 4

Flatulence, Favism and Other Factors

Legumes are one of nature's most perfect foods—wonderfully nutritious. Just don't go overboard, though, and suddenly load up on beans and peas. For one thing, any large increase in fiber can create a medley of problems: cut down your absorption of minerals, cause flatulence, cramps and even intestinal blockage.

Flatulence

Some people say they avoid eating beans because the biggest bugbear about eating them is the gas—a bloated feeling and increased flatulence. As the children's cheeky rhyme goes:

"Beans, beans, the musical fruit.
The more you eat, the more you toot."

So what causes it? And, more to the point, what can you do about it? Plenty.

The topic of gas and flatulence is an embarrassing one for many people; it's euphemistically referred to as gastric distress, and not much talked about. But the truth is that we naturally have gas in our intestinal tract and release it one way or another. How much gas does your body normally produce? We are all different. You may produce anywhere between 400 cc to 2,400 cc of *flatus* each day, depending on how much air you swallow and certain foods in your diet.

You swallow air each time you eat, sip hot drinks slowly, or gulp bubbly beverages such as beer, soda or fizzy bottled water. Gas accumulates in the stomach, to be belched out or to pass into the small intestine where part of it is absorbed. Some gas diffuses through the intestinal wall into the blood stream and is then carried to the lungs and exhaled in the breath. The rest travels into the colon to be passed out through the rectum.

Foods such as cooked dried beans, peas, cauliflower, brussels sprouts, broccoli, cabbage and bran can be troublesome gas-makers because they are not completely digested in the small intestine. By the time the undigested pieces of food reach the colon, they arrive in a form that the body cannot absorb—mainly cellulose and oligosaccharides (carbohydrates containing two to eight sugar molecules, mostly *raffinose, stachyose* and *verbacose*). The intestinal tract doesn't produce enzymes capable of splitting these oligosaccharides, so the large population of colon bacteria goes to work on these complex sugars with fermentation, and this process often gives off various gases (primarily carbon dioxide and hydrogen, and odoriferous ones such as hydrogen sulfide—the bad-egg odor) as waste products.

Who is affected? If you don't often eat beans, gas is more likely to be a nuisance when you do. If you are unaccustomed to large portions of beans or peas on a daily basis, they can leave you feeling stuffed or bloated. A few people never get used to eating beans, while others never have to make any adjustments. People in countries such as India, Africa and South America (and similar ethnic groups in the USA) who regularly eat beans, seem to have less trouble with flatulence. Maybe their digestive tracts have adapted to diets rich in beans, or maybe gas formation is discouraged by life-styles of hard physical labor such as farm work and cultivating crops.

What you can do

Don't assume you're going to have a gas problem with beans just because someone you know is affected. Consult your doctor about the problem and the usual advice is to avoid eating gas-producing foods; but this can mean giving up most of the foods now being promoted as important to health. Your doctor may want to perform tests to make sure you have no abnormalities in your digestive tract, or suggest you need only take simethicone. But if symptoms are not severe, most people find effective relief with a few simple changes, such as:

Small portions. The digestive system works best if you let it adapt slowly to any change in diet. The idea is to introduce beans and peas (and other high-fiber foods) gradually and in small portions. Don't mix beans with other gaseous vegetables such as cabbage at the same meal, until your system can accommodate them comfortably and get used to the extra fiber load. It also helps to drink more liquids and get more exercise. In this way, many people make the adjustment after about three weeks.

Which beans? Different kinds of beans vary in their ability to produce gas, and the good news is that some of the "new" beans have reduced amounts of the gas-producers. Generally, Anasazi and tepary beans, fresh young peas and immature green beans give the least trouble; the worst offenders are limas and navy beans which can be powerful producers of gas. Colorado State University has studied Anasazis versus pintos, and reports that Anasazi beans contain less than 25% of the carbohydrates responsible for gastric distress:

	Anasazi	Pinto
Raffinose	0.36	1.37
Stachyose	0.11	0.55
Verbacose	0.04	0.21
Total	0.51	2.13
Ratio	1.00 :	4.18

The right preparation. When you cook dried beans from scratch, you can lessen gas discomfort in two ways: first, *never* cook beans in their soak-water, and second, cook them *thoroughly*.

1. Soak them in unsalted water for at least four hours before cooking (using three or four times as much water as beans), changing and discarding the water several times during soaking. The soaking process helps to leach out the complex sugars we can't digest. Rinse and stir the soaked beans in a colander under cold running water, drain well and return to pan. Then cover with fresh unsalted water (again, three to four times as much water as beans), bring to a boil, place the lid on the saucepan and reduce to a simmer. Some cooks add a small amount of sodium bicarbonate (baking soda), but this can destroy some thiamin and leave a soapy flavor.

2. Be sure legumes are completely cooked. While you might enjoy the crunch of raw or lightly cooked vegetables and pasta served *al dente*, the starches in beans do need thorough cooking for better digestibility.

You may find that cooked *canned* beans are less troublesome to your stomach; just be sure to rinse and drain them well to take out any excess salt before using in recipes.

Herbs and spices. How do people in other countries fight bean-related flatulence? Very often they add herbs or spices. *Ginger,* the well-known spice derived from *Zingiber officinale*, has proved to be superior medicine for stomach problems including flatulence. If you are unable to buy the various preparations of ginger in health-food stores, the ginger powder and fresh ginger from supermarkets can be equally effective. Fresh ginger, sometimes known as ginger "root," has a potato-like skin; you need to peel it before chopping or grating it into a pot of beans or split peas.

In Mexico, cooks wouldn't think of boiling up a pot of black beans without using the pungent herb *epazote* *(Chenopodium ambrosioides),* which effectively prevents flatulence and imparts a distinctive spiciness similar to cilantro. In central and southern Mexico, fresh leaves of this herb are used in cooking pots. In the United States you can probably find the dried herb in health-food stores or Hispanic markets under a variety of names: lamb's quarters, goosefoot, Mexican tea, wormseed and Jerusalem oak. One sprig of fresh *epazote* or $1/2$ teaspoon of the dried herb is about right for most recipes, added just before the end of cooking time.

In India, *asafetida* is used not only as a digestive aid to ward off flatulence and colic, but is also prized for its truffle-like flavor. It is always put into pots of dried beans, lentils and split peas. You can buy it in Indian markets, sold either as a small lump or as a grainy powder. Make your own powder, if you like, by splitting off a small piece of *asafetida* (about the size of a green pea, for most recipes) and crushing it between two sheets of paper.

Charcoal. Activated charcoal capsules (for instance, *Charcocaps* by Requa, sold without prescription in drugstores, or other brands in health-food stores) taken before or soon after a bean meal can greatly reduce intestinal gas, and give bean eaters fewer problems with bloating and flatulence. But charcoal is not a perfect solution, because you need to take a lot of it (four large capsules before and four after eating troublesome beans), and the cost of charcoal can make it prohibitively expensive, since 36 capsules sell for about $5. Another drawback with charcoal is that it doesn't discriminate among the compounds it blocks so it can also cut down absorption in the intestines of mineral nutrients in food or health supplements and any drugs you're taking.

The new gas preventive. For bean lovers who hate gas, AkPharma, Inc. has formulated an innovative anti-gas product: an enzyme with the tongue-twisting name *alpha-galactosidase,* appropriately dubbed Beano,™ that digests the gas-producing compounds in foods such as beans, peas, broccoli, cabbage and onions. Most gas relievers work by reducing stomach or intestinal gas after it has already formed, but this enzyme works in a different way, making vegetable and legume sugars digestible as you eat them.

You don't cook with Beano, as the product is inactivated at high temperatures, but stir it in at serving time. Simply add three to eight drops of the liquid to the first bite of an individual serving of beans (or other gas-producing vegetables) and the enzyme works in the stomach by breaking down the non-digestible sugars into sugars that can be absorbed by the body. It tastes somewhat like soy sauce, slightly salty— although there are only 12 mg of sodium in 5 drops. Beano is sold without prescription, and is available in pharmacies, health-food stores and supermarkets.

One caution: since it's derived from a food-grade fungus, *Aspergillus niger*, Beano is classified as a food product and not a drug, but if you have any mold allergies that cause breathing problems, you should check first with your doctor before using it.

Favism

Another problem associated with eating beans can be more serious: favism, which is an inherited disorder involving an allergy-like reaction to eating fava (broad) beans. Although rare in most of the world, it is common among people with ancestors from the Mediterranean (Spaniards, Italians, Greeks, Sardinians, Armenians, Kurds and Sephardic Jews), about 10 percent of American blacks (those with West African roots), as well as Taiwanese and Thais.

The favism factor (a sensitivity to the fava bean toxin *vicine*) causes a breakdown of red blood cells, triggering anemia and jaundice, with the anemia severe enough to cause weakness, vertigo, headaches, tinnitus, spots before the eyes, fatigue, drowsiness and irritability. It appears that susceptible people have red blood cells deficient in G-6-PD (Glucose-6-Phosphate Dehydrogenase)—an inherited deficiency believed to provide protection against some forms of malaria. These people may suffer from favism after eating undercooked fava beans, and even be sensitive to the flower pollen from these beans if, for instance, they happen to walk through a field where favas are growing.

The ancient Egyptians, Greeks and Romans knew about the trouble: the aristocrats of those times disdained legumes and considered them "poor man's meat" because some people became sick after eating them. They didn't know *why* they suffered but they had their superstitions. As long ago as 500 B.C., Egyptians thought fava beans unclean and caused nightmares or insomnia. Herodotus wrote that Egyptian priests were forbidden to eat favas: "They cannot even bear to look at them because they imagine they are unclean." The philosopher Pythagoras forbade his followers to eat them because he believed that beans contained the souls of the dead. The Romans ate them, even though they considered favas to be unlucky.

What you can do

If you have this family background (other people are *not* affected), it's best to be aware of the risk and avoid eating beans in this group, that is: fava (broad) beans, lupines and bell beans (*ful nabed*). There are many wonderful beans that *don't* cause favism, so you are better off to substitute other varieties.

Other Factors
That Can Be Somewhat Harmful

Certain beans and peas can have other substances that are anti-nutritional or toxic, although when you prepare legumes properly they shouldn't cause any difficulty.

Certain varieties of lima beans contain *cyanogens* which have caused serious cases of cyanide poisoning in the tropics. However, American and European plant breeders have now developed low-cyanogen varieties and most developed countries have laws that restrict commercial lima bean production to the safest types. Still, it's a good rule: *never eat raw beans.* The potentially toxic compounds in those beans are easily removed if you soak and thoroughly boil dried lima beans in an uncovered pot: hydrogen cyanide gas forms and escapes with the steam. When limas are raw and green, or have been sprouted, roasted or boiled in a covered saucepan, they are probably not harmful if you eat them only in small amounts.

Beans are the most common food group to contain

classes of molecules called *protease inhibitors* and *lectins*. Protease inhibitors can be troublesome because they interfere with digestion of proteins, and can also affect the pancreas, overstimulating it to produce more and more enzymes. The toxins called lectins affect the intestines and prevent the absorption of nutrients; they can cause stomach cramps, nausea and diarrhea. Fortunately they are made harmless by boiling temperatures—lower cooking temperatures don't work.

Peas *(Pisum sativum)* and beans in the kidney family *(Phaseolus vulgaris)* should not be eaten raw. They can interfere with the action of vitamin E and damage the liver and muscles. Raw peas and soybeans can also bind essential metals such as copper, iron, manganese and zinc so that the body can't use them in metabolism; and eating too many soybeans can increase your need for vitamins A, B_{12} and D, and dietary iodine—although these factors can be counteracted in part by cooking, roasting or pressure cooking.

However, in spite of the drawbacks, there's no doubt that beans are terrific for bringing wonderful nutrition to vegetarian meals—and the new varieties add excitement. Let's start cooking!

CHAPTER 5

Bean Basics

Why are the least expensive foods the most fun to cook? Spend a dollar or two on a pound of dried beans or peas, and you have a wonderfully simple food that is not only amazingly satisfying and nourishing, but also entertaining to prepare and serve. Beans can be child's play to cook—and in fact, they are a good way to start youngsters on their first lessons in food preparation in the kitchen. At the same time, beans have a versatility to challenge and inspire the inventive and experienced cook. This versatility allows beans and peas to combine with any number of culinary companions, to switch and change recipes to suit pocketbooks, family preferences and stylish parties. Although beans have a traditional down-to-earth heartiness, the unusual and special varieties present a simple sophistication when partnered with exotic dishes on a menu. Now starring in trendy restaurants, elegant at-home brunches and easy family suppers, legumes are showing up in hearty winter soups and stuffings, cool summer-time salads, and around-the-calendar sandwiches and snacks.

Where to buy bean varieties

Several kinds belong in any well-stocked pantry, and you'll want to try the exciting varieties now taking center stage.

If you're a newcomer to beans, visit the bean aisle at the market to start buying one or two different types. Packages of dried kidney, navy, pinto and black beans, chickpeas, split peas and lentils are usually found in the dry-bean sections of grocery and health-food stores and supermarkets, alongside the dried pastas. For can-opener cooks, canned cooked beans packed in several container sizes are normally available in the canned vegetable section of the store. The frozen food cabinets usually stock packs of crowders, black-eyes and limas.

If you have trouble finding the particular bean needed for a special recipe, ask the store manager about placing an order for that variety. Perhaps other customers have requested it too. Knowing the various colloquial names for each bean can be useful (many are detailed in Appendix 1), since stores in your region or local neighborhood may call them something different.

To locate other varieties of dried beans or canned beans, you may need to go further afield, but first check your local health-food or natural-food stores, ethnic food stores (such as Indian, Latino or Chinese), or those sections of your supermarket. Because beans are used often in ethnic cuisines, the turnover is quicker and the dried beans tend to be younger. Old beans languishing on a store shelf will take longer soaking and cooking.

Dozens of unusual varieties of good quality dried legumes are easily available by mail order, phone or FAX, from specialty food stores that feature heirloom beans, listed in Appendix 2.

Buying good beans

When you buy dried beans, check the package to ensure that the beans are firm, whole, clean, and of uniform size and color. Although some varieties, such as large limas, are more vulnerable to being broken in pieces or having broken skins, this condition doesn't usually affect flavor or wholesomeness; but, obviously, perfect whole beans make dishes such as salads more attractive and appealing.

The thrifty gourmet can save by buying loose beans, but they need to be closely examined. Bulk beans are no bargain if they appear to have tiny holes—they may have been improperly stored and allowed to harbor small bugs and weevils, not often found in commercial packages.

Storage

Dry beans can be stored a long time (but not forever!) if you keep them in their sealed unopened plastic packages. When you buy loose beans, or break open a package, you need to transfer them to tightly covered glass or metal containers and store in a cool dry place—but not the refrigerator.

A good idea is to pack each variety in large airtight screw-top jars—clean and dry mayonnaise jars are a handy size. Why not brighten your kitchen counter with a collection of glass jars containing the new jazzy multicolored beans?—they're perfect in a country kitchen and can enliven the austere look of a townhouse.

Don't be tempted to toss old and new purchases or different varieties together, as the length of soaking and cooking times can vary. Mark the date of purchase on the jar label, and use beans in rotation, moving the oldest ones to the front and cooking them first. Beans will keep their quality for six to twelve months if you store them this way, but the longer they are stored, the more they will pick up moisture or dryness from their surroundings. When beans absorb or lose moisture, the times for soaking and cooking will change; if exposed to high temperatures and humidity, beans can be difficult to cook.

Unopened *canned* beans should be stored, like other canned foods, in a dry place away from heat, with moderate temperatures below 70 degrees F (21 degrees C), and above freezing. Mark the date of purchase on the cans, and use them in rotation, using the oldest first. Opened cans containing unused portions can be stored, covered, in the refrigerator for up to four days.

Drain leftover beans and cool them rapidly, uncovered, then cover for refrigerating or freezing. Pack cooked beans, mashed beans and bean leftovers in covered containers, and refrigerate for up to four days; for longer storage, they freeze well without loss of quality for up to six months. It's handy to store them in recipe-sized quantities.

When packing beans for freezing, they can be slightly undercooked, because freezing tends to soften them; allow room for expansion in the container. Defrost frozen beans slowly overnight in the refrigerator to retain their shape; or thaw for several hours at room temperature. If you're in a real hurry, they will defrost in about an hour in a pan of warm water, or within minutes in the microwave.

Preparation, sorting and rinsing

Although farmers and processors put beans through threshers and sifters, all dried beans, peas and lentils need a careful examination in the kitchen before preparing.

Spread them out on an tray in a well-lighted spot where you can pick them over thoroughly with a sharp eye, making sure to discard all pieces of dirt, perilous pebbles and other foreign material that escaped the cleaning equipment. Throw out any misshaped or damaged beans. Be extra careful with smaller beans such as pinquitos, teparies, lentils and chickpeas bought in bulk as they can easily conceal small stones that would wreak havoc with dental work. Better to spot them now rather than let them damage teeth at mealtime.

Before packaging, beans are not usually washed because moisture would make them start to sprout, so when you're ready to soak and cook them, you'll need to remove field dust by swishing the beans in a colander under running cold water.

Don't mix

Cooking beans with similar cooking times in the same pot is not a good idea. Their flavors and colors will mingle and lack distinction, and any unknown or unseen differences in age and dryness will produce uneven cooking—some may cook perfectly, others may disintegrate to mush and the rest remain obstinately hard.

To soak or not to soak

Many cooks say they've been cooking beans for years without bothering about soaking, and the discussion continues as to whether beans should be soaked and, if so, which way is right. It's true that split peas and lentils need only to be washed before they are cooked, but the recommendation here is that most whole beans and whole peas want a water-soak after washing. Why?, you ask. Because beans must rehydrate before they can begin to cook. A dried bean has a moisture content of only about 15 percent, and after fully cooking, about 60 percent, so it needs to absorb plenty of water. Beans have skins that water can't easily penetrate, except at the *hilum*, where the bean or pea was attached to the pod. When you rehydrate the interior of the bean under the skin, you reduce cooking time (thus saving energy expense), and the cooking will give each bean a uniform texture. Each one will hold its shape better and keep a smooth skin. If your dried legumes come directly from the specialist-bean farm, soaking can be minimal, but long soaking is recommended particularly for old beans and tough-skinned fava beans and for the denser varieties such as the kidneys, pinks, pinquitos and small whites. Soaking may fade some bean colors and cause paler markings in speckled, mottled or veined beans.

Another major advantage to soaking beans is that if you use the preferred overnight hot-soak plan described below, and pour off the soak water, you reduce the digestive problems that beans are noted for. While beans are soaking for four hours or more, much of the indigestible sugars which cause many people to have gas are dissolved and discarded when the soak water is thrown away. Some purists argue that discarding the soak water means losing valuable bean nutrients, but food researchers consider the amounts of lost nutrients insignificant. Beans still retain all the good protein, carbohydrate and fiber that are the main nutritional reasons why people eat beans. For most people, avoiding indigestion is more important than losing trace amounts of nutrients that can be obtained from other food.

Whichever plan you use, be sure to drain away the soak water and rinse the beans, in case the water has developed a sour flavor.

You can use a couple of soaking methods: the Overnight hot-soak plan or the Quick-soak plan:

Overnight hot-soak plan: Sort beans and wash in a colander. In a large pot (beans will expand to over twice their dry volume), add 10 cups of hot water for each one pound of dried beans, any variety. Cover and let stand overnight or about 8 hours, stirring occasionally. (Soybeans need to be refrigerated while soaking, to avert fermentation.) Discard and replace the soak water a few times, if you can, then finally rinse and drain the beans. This is an important step.

Quick-soak plan: Sort beans and wash in a colander. In a large pot add 10 cups of hot water for each one pound of dried beans. Bring to a boil and cook for 2 or 3 minutes, then remove from heat, cover and let stand for at least one hour—preferably four hours. The longer you can soak the beans, the greater amount of sugars will dissolve, making the beans more digestible. Discard the soak water; then rinse and drain the beans.

An important fact

Never eat raw beans or peas. All dried beans, peas and lentils must be boiled before you eat them. These legumes contain lectins, toxins which can cause nausea, stomach cramps and diarrhea (see Chapter 4). Water must be boiling to destroy lectins; lower temperatures won't work. Peas and lentils have a low level of lectins and need only to be brought to a brief boil before cooking with a gentle heat. Most beans are high in lectins, and must be boiled for 10 minutes before simmering.

Cooking beans...

How you cook beans can depend on the type of bean you are using, the amount of time you have, or available cooking utensils. Dry beans can be cooked conventionally on the stove-top, in a crock pot, a pressure cooker or zapped in the microwave.

...On the stove-top

For simple boiled beans as a hot vegetable or for casseroles: place the beans (soaked, rinsed and drained) in a large saucepan with fresh hot water to about one inch above the beans. For each pound of beans add a tablespoon of cooking oil to reduce foaming and boil-overs;

olive oil, butter or bacon drippings can be used, if you want those more distinctive flavors. Boil for 10 minutes then simmer until tender. Tilt the pot lid, if foaming becomes a problem—some bean varieties create more froth than others. Stir the beans occasionally to prevent sticking, and add extra hot water if needed to keep beans just covered with liquid. Simmer gently to prevent skins from bursting.

Add seasonings during this cooking time, if you like. For a delicious deep savory flavor, especially if you want beans to star as a side dish or salad, toss in a whole onion and a couple of garlic cloves (which can be lifted out before serving). Add 1/4 teaspoon mustard, 1/4 teaspoon white pepper and 1 tablespoon vegetable stock base (or 2 or 3 bouillon cubes). Unsalted broth left over from cooking vegetables can make a lovely savory substitute instead of water. Or you can season with 2 teaspoons onion powder, 1/4 teaspoon garlic powder, some finely chopped celery, chopped fresh parsley or dried herbs, bay leaf and spices.

Don't add salt, garlic salt, onion salt or acidic ingredients such as tomatoes, ketchup, chili sauce, lemon juice, vinegar or wine, until *after* the beans are tender at the end of the cooking time. Salt and acid will toughen the skins and they never will become tender—no matter how long you boil them. Similarly, if your recipe includes molasses, add it during the later stages as the trace of calcium in molasses can also harden bean skins.

...In the pressure cooker

Some pressure-cooker manufacturers think dried beans are "forbidden foods" since frothing action or a loose bean skin lodged in the vent can clog it. Some beans, especially soybeans, can be troublesome when their foam bubbles up through the pressure valve while cooking, but with a little care you shouldn't have difficulty, and these cookers are a great way to save time. (And if you are too rushed to pre-soak beans, you can merely add 5 to 20 minutes to the normal cooking period.)

Place the rinsed, soaked, drained beans in the pressure cooker and add water to cover plus 1 tablespoon of cooking oil or butter for each cup of dried beans to prevent foaming. To avoid the possibility of a clogged vent, it's important not to fill the cooker more than one-third full of ingredients including soaked beans and cooking liquid. Cover and cook at 10 pounds pressure about 20 minutes, or according to the times given for specific varieties in Appendix 1, or check your manufacturer's instructions. Be careful not to overcook.

If you should hear loud sputtering while cooking beans (unlikely), place the cooker under cold running water to quickly reduce pressure. Remove and clean the lid, vent and rubber gasket. Re-lock the lid in place and proceed with cooking.

At the end of cooking time, quick-release the pressure by running cold water over the pressure-cooker lid to avoid sputtering at the vent. After cooking beans, always clean the lid and vent thoroughly: pass a strong jet of water through the valve orifice to clear it of any obstructions.

...In the crock pot

Place the rinsed, soaked, drained beans in a saucepan with boiling water to cover and simmer for 10 minutes. Then place beans in the crock pot and add 6 cups of water per one pound of beans. Cook on low setting for about 12 hours or until done, or use manufacturer's directions.

...In the microwave oven

You can use the microwave for soaking, cooking and thawing frozen beans, heating canned beans (after transferring them to microwaveable dishes), reheating or finishing prepared recipes.

Because all microwave ovens are not created equal, it's a good idea to check the manufacturer's directions developed for your microwave. Just as microwave ovens vary in size, shape and color, their cooking power or wattage varies from oven to oven, and wattage will affect the cooking times of beans. Microwave recipes are generally developed for 600- to 700-watt ovens. If your oven is less than 600 watts, you'll need to compensate by adding extra time to each step of the cooking instructions.

Although the overnight soaking method is preferable, the microwave is handy for quick soaking: put one pound of washed beans in a 5-quart glass container with 8 cups of water. Cover with an all-glass lid or plastic wrap, then cook at full power for 8 to 10 minutes or until boiling. Let stand for 1 hour or longer, stirring occasionally, then drain.

To cook one pound of beans, add 6 to 8 cups of fresh hot water, cover and cook at full power for 15 minutes or until boiling; stir; reduce to medium power (50 percent) and cook another 15 to 20 minutes or until beans are tender. Stir once again, then let stand 5 minutes to finish the cooking process.

To complete a casserole or main dish, layer or mix ingredients in a glass or china dish, cover with a glass lid or plastic wrap, and cook at medium setting (50 percent) until all ingredients are blended, hot and bubbly. Allow the dish to stand 5 minutes.

Bean leftovers frozen in plastic boxes can thaw in minutes in the microwave, letting you put them on the table in record time. The microwave reheats frozen beans beautifully because the risk of scorching or pan-sticking is minimized. Twelve ounces of mashed cooked beans will defrost on a medium-low setting in about 5 minutes. Stir halfway through, then let stand for 5 minutes. To revive flavor and consistency after thawing, you might like to add a little broth or extra seasoning.

How long do you cook beans?

Accurate timing is impossible to give because of many variables such as the bean variety, the age of the beans, the hardness of your water supply, and your altitude (more about that later). Fortunately cooking times for beans are not quite as critical as they are with fresh vegetables. There's more leeway with beans, so an extra minute or two is unlikely to turn them into mush.

When considering cooking times, think of the use you intend to make of the beans: when you need beans for salads, or freezing for later use, or if they will be cooked further in soups, stews or casseroles, you generally want them firm-cooked or slightly under-cooked. For purées, smooth soups, sauces, dips or mashed beans, a longer time works best, until the beans are soft.

Old beans that have suffered lengthy storage will probably take longer to cook than the new season's supplies coming directly from the farm or ranch (or newly dried from your own garden produce). As a general rule, colored and mottled beans take longer to cook than white, except navy and small whites; lentils cook rapidly. Follow the times for specific and unusual varieties in Appendix 1; a few of the commonly-sold beans are given here:

Black-eyes	30 mins. to 1 hour
Chickpeas	1 to $1\frac{1}{2}$ hours
Kidneys, pinks, small whites	1 to $1\frac{1}{2}$ hours
Limas: baby	1 hour
large	45 mins. to 1 hour

When are beans tender?

Since cooking times can only be approximate, the best idea is to test frequently during cooking. Test for doneness by squeezing a whole bean or pea between your fingers, or tasting a small spoonful of purée—but take care if it's hot! Otherwise you can press a bean on a cutting board with a fork, which will avoid burning your tongue. Let beans cool in their cooking liquid to keep skins intact.

How do you make a purée?

For smooth soups, velvety sauces and gravies, and other dishes that specify bean purée: soak overnight $\frac{1}{2}$ pound (one cup) dry beans, rinse and drain. Cook with fresh water until extremely tender and mushy. Drain off and reserve cooking liquid. Put beans in a food blender, one cup at a time, with $\frac{1}{4}$ cup of the reserved cooking liquid, and spin at medium setting until smooth. Occasionally stop the blender to stir purée from the bottom and to scrape the sides of the container.

What can you do when beans won't cook?

If your beans don't cook to the tender stage within the expected time, there could be several reasons:

1. Did you add salt, acidic ingredients or molasses too soon, instead of at the end of cooking time?

2. Do you have hard water? Water that contains a high proportion of calcium and magnesium can toughen bean skins before the starches are softened, and prolong cooking time in the same way as salt and acids. To avoid this problem, you can use purified bottled drinking water for the bean liquid. Although some cooks add $\frac{1}{8}$ teaspoon of baking soda to the soaking and cooking liquid to overcome hard-water problems, the soda can give a soapy taste to delicately flavored beans and change the texture.

3. Do you live at an altitude above 3,500 feet? Cooking takes longer than normal because water will boil at lower temperatures. To avoid this snag, you can simply plan ahead by allowing extra cooking time, or alternatively prepare them in a pressure cooker.

How much to cook?

Let's play the numbers game and do a little arithmetic:

1 cup uncooked dry beans	= about $2\frac{1}{2}$ to 3 cups when cooked
1 cup uncooked dry beans	= about 4 servings when cooked
1 lb uncooked dry beans	= 2 cups dry
	= 5 to 6 cups when cooked
	= about 9 servings of baked beans
	= about 12 servings of bean soup

For can-opener cooks:

16 oz can = $15\frac{1}{2}$ oz when drained = $1\frac{2}{3}$ cup cooked beans

Cooking for the crowd

Perhaps you're hosting a big fund-raising barbecue, planning the family reunion, doing catering, or are in charge of the school lunch program. Here are some larger numbers that will come in handy. When rounding up larger cooking vessels, be sure to reckon their weight when full of beans and cooking liquid; several smaller pans may be easier to lift and carry. After 1 lb of dried beans is cooked, the weight is about $2\frac{1}{2}$ lbs; when 8 lbs of dried beans are cooked, the weight is about 20 lbs.

Ingredient	25 servings	50 servings
Dry beans	4 lbs	8 lbs
Water	1½ gals	3 gals
Oil or margarine	½ cup (1 stick)	1 cup (2 sticks)
Whole onions, chopped	2	4
Garlic cloves, minced	2	4
Celery, diced	1 cup	2 cups
Parsley, fresh, chopped	¼ cup	½ cup
Bay leaves, whole, dried	2	4
Pepper	1 tablespoon	2 tablespoons
Dry mustard	1 tablespoon	2 tablespoons
Cooking time	1½ to 2 hours	1½ to 2 hours
Salt (added after cooking)	1½ tablespoons	3 tablespoons
Yield	about 1½ gals	about 3 to 3¼ gals
Weight after cooking	10 lbs	20 lbs

Kitchen Conversion Charts

Volume:

U.S. Measure	U.S. fluid ounces	Imperial fluid ounces	Metric milliliters
1 teaspoon	¼	¼	5
1 tablespoon	½	½	15
2 tablespoons	1	1	30
¼ cup	2	2	60
⅓ cup	3	3	90
½ cup	4	4	120
⅔ cup	5	5 (¼ pint)	145
¾ cup	6	6	175
1 cup	8	8	235
1 pint	16	16½	475
1 quart	32	33	945
1 gallon	128	133	1.89 liters

U.S. fluid ounce	= 29.6 ml	Imperial fluid ounce = 28.4 ml
U.S. standard cup = 8 fl oz		Imperial standard cup = 10 fl oz
U.S. pint = 16 fl oz		Imperial pint = 20 fl oz

Weight:

U.S./Imperial ounces	Metric grams
½	14
1	28
2	57
3	85
4	113
5	142
6	170
7	198
8	227
12	340
16 (1 lb)	454

Oven temperatures:

Fahrenheit	Centigrade	British Gas Mark	Heat Level
225	110	¼	very cool
250	130	½	very cool
275	140	1	cool or slow
300	150	·2	cool or slow
325	170	3	warm
350	180	4	moderate
375	190	5	moderately hot
400	200	6	fairly hot
425	220	7	hot
450	230	8	very hot
475	240	9	very hot

CHAPTER 6

New Bean Recipes

These recipes contain no meat, fish or poultry. The stocks and gravies have been created from vegetable stock or water flavored with vegetarian bouillon. However, whole eggs, milk, whole-milk cheeses and other milk products have been used.

For a vegan (a vegetarian who excludes eggs or dairy products), or a person concerned with cholesterol intake, other ingredients can be substituted:

Butter: Vegans will naturally use vegetable margarine.

Cheese: Health-food stores and some large supermarkets offer nondairy rennet-free cheese. There are excellent tofu and soy cheeses available in many varieties. Most soy cheese has a mild cheese flavor, a slight rubbery texture, and melting qualities similar, but not identical, to dairy cheese.

Eggs: Tofu or a powdered eggless product, found in most health-food stores and some supermarkets, can be interchanged with the eggs used in recipes. Check packages for directions.

Milk: "Plain" (unflavored or original) soy milk, available at most supermarkets, can be used for milk and milk products. However, for most recipes, soy milk needs thickening with a *roux* made of flour or corn-starch to produce the consistency of dairy milk.

Sour cream: An alternative is vegetable-based sour cream, available in supermarkets and health-food stores.

Yogurt: Health-food stores usually stock nondairy soy-based yogurt substitutes.

Appetizers

These can be interesting starters to a complete lovely meal, or can serve as simple snacks when a few friends come over for drinks and a small bite to eat.

When beans need to be mashed or puréed, they should be well cooked and extremely tender.

Bean-Stuffed Dolmas
Black Bean Pizza
Cheesy Bean Puffies
Falafel Balls
Hummus Middle East Dip
Mexican Bean Dip
Nigerian Akara Balls
Party Paté
South American Popcorn
Swedish Mushroom Caps
Vegetable Pizza

Bean-Stuffed Dolmas

Dolmas (from the Turkish *dolma* = stuffed) are popular in many Middle Eastern countries. Made from grape leaves or cabbage leaves, or maybe a vegetable shell such as halved green bell pepper, eggplant or zucchini, they are usually stuffed with meat, rice, nuts, etc. In Iran and India, cooks like to include currants and cinnamon. This delicious recipe is in the Greek style.

> 1 (8-oz) jar grape leaves
> $\frac{1}{2}$ cup cooked and mashed cannellini beans
> 1 cup cooked short brown rice
> $\frac{1}{4}$ cup diced walnuts
> $\frac{1}{2}$ medium onion, grated
> 2 garlic cloves, mashed
> $\frac{1}{4}$ teaspoon salt
> 1 tablespoon olive oil
> 1 tablespoon lemon juice

Remove grape leaves from jar, wash and leave to drain.

Mix other ingredients, except lemon juice, together in a bowl.

To assemble: take 20 leaves and place stem-side up. Snip stem off each leaf. Put 1 teaspoon of filling near stem end. Bring left side of leaf towards center, then bring right side towards center (they don't always meet). Pick up stem end of leaf, tucking in the filling. Roll away from you to make an oblong roll like a little log. When all the rolls are assembled, place them in a steamer basket, with water and 1 tablespoon lemon juice in the lower pan.

Steam 10 minutes.

Makes about 20 appetizers.

Black Bean Pizza

Everybody loves pizza, traditionally made with cheese and tomato sauce, but black beans make this one really special.

Pizza crust
> 1 cup all-purpose flour
> 1 teaspoon baking powder
> $\frac{1}{2}$ teaspoon salt
> $\frac{1}{3}$ cup milk
> 1 tablespoon oil

Mix all ingredients in a bowl and stir until mixture leaves the sides. Press into a ball and knead about ten times until smooth. Roll out a 13-inch circle on a floured board. Place on a 10-inch pan and pinch up sides all around. Now prepare topping.

Topping
> 1 medium onion
> 2 tablespoons oil
> 1 (8-oz) can tomato sauce
> 2 teaspoons garlic powder
> 1 teaspoon oregano
> $\frac{1}{2}$ cup shredded mozzarella cheese
> $\frac{1}{2}$ cup freshly grated Parmesan cheese
> $\frac{1}{2}$ cup cooked Black Valentine, turtle or black beans, drained
> 1 teaspoon fennel seeds (optional)

Slice onion and sauté in oil until translucent. Set aside. Mix tomato sauce, garlic powder and oregano together and, using the back of a spoon, spread evenly over dough. Sprinkle cheeses and sautéed onions over mixture, and then beans and fennel seeds. Bake at 425 degrees F for 20 to 25 minutes until bubbly. Cut into pie-shaped wedges and serve hot.

Makes a 10-inch round pizza.

Cheesy Bean Puffies

These mouth-watering puffs will make your cocktail party a success. They can be made with many varieties of beans and cheese, including soy cheese.

1 can (10 count) buttermilk baking-powder biscuits
$\frac{1}{2}$ cup American, Velveeta, or any processed
    Cheddar-flavored cheese
2 tablespoons butter or margarine
$\frac{1}{3}$ cup cooked white kidney beans, mashed

Separate the biscuits and cut each one into quarters. Place on a well-greased cookie sheet. Melt cheese and butter together. Top each biscuit quarter with $\frac{1}{4}$ teaspoon of mashed beans then spoon melted cheese mixture on top, spreading down the sides.

Bake at 350 degrees F for 10 to 15 minutes till toasty yellow and puffy. Serve hot.

Makes 40 puffs.

Falafel Balls

This is an authentic Israeli recipe. Serve these balls with tahini sauce (bought at health-food stores), a honey mustard, or a hot and spicy chili sauce, to accent the Mediterranean touch.

1 lb garbanzos, cooked and drained
3 slices bread
1/4 cup onion, chopped
2 garlic cloves
3 small sprigs fresh parsley
3 eggs, beaten
1/2 teaspoon salt
3 good turns of a black pepper mill
Oil for frying (preferably peanut oil, to add a nutty
    flavor)

In food processor process beans, bread, onion, garlic and parsley. Put in a medium bowl and add beaten eggs, salt and pepper. Let stand about 1 hour. In a fry pan pour oil to about 1/2″ to 1″ depth. When oil is hot, make the falafel into balls, round but flat enough to fry. Fry in oil till crisp and brown on both sides. Drain well and pierce each with a toothpick. Serve hot with one of the above sauces.

Makes 18 to 24 cocktail size balls.

Hummus
Middle East Dip

Serve this dip with pieces of pita bread, Armenian bread or sesame crackers. It's also very good with raw vegetables. You can buy tahini, which is ground sesame seeds, in some supermarkets, health-food stores and specialty stores.

> 1 cup cooked, drained and cooled garbanzos (chick peas)
> 2 tablespoons chopped fresh parsley
> 1 to $1\frac{1}{2}$ tablespoons tahini
> 1 tablespoon lemon juice
> 1 tablespoon olive oil
> 2 garlic cloves
> Additional chopped fresh parsley for garnish

Place all ingredients in a food processor and whirl until smooth and well blended. If too thick, thin with about $\frac{1}{4}$ cup water. Spoon into a pretty serving bowl, cover and refrigerate for at least 1 hour. Serve at room temperature, garnished with a sprinkling of parsley.

Makes about 1½ cups.

Mexican Bean Dip

This bean dip is perfect for a between-meal snack or for an appetizer before dinner. For a quick open-face hot sandwich, spread the dip on slices of sourdough bread, top with a sprinkling of grated Jack or Cheddar cheese. Slip it under the broiler until cheese melts and sandwich is heated through.

> 2 cups cooked turtle beans, drained
> 4 scallions, chopped
> $\frac{1}{2}$ cup vegetarian broth (or 1 vegetarian bouillon cube
>   dissolved in $\frac{1}{2}$ cup water)
> 3 tablespoons diced green chilis
> $\frac{1}{2}$ cup sour cream
> 1 garlic clove
> Salt and freshly ground black pepper to taste
> $\frac{1}{2}$ avocado, cubed (optional)

Process all ingredients except avocado in a food processor. Add more sour cream, if necessary. Place in serving bowl, garnished with avocado cubes on top. Serve with Bean Chips™ tortilla chips, crisp jicama or other raw vegetables.

Makes about 3 cups.

Nigerian Akara Balls

This tempting appetizer originated in West Africa where cooks use the indigenous black-eyed peas. The black-eyed pea fritter sold on the streets in Nigeria as *akara* (or *akla*) is without doubt the same *acaraje* found in Brazil. Acaraje fried to a golden crisp in palm oil by local black women in the State of Bahia is an emblem of the slave experience in the New World, and probably related to the *akkra* in Trinidad and *acrat* in the French islands of the Caribbean. If you'd like this dish to have a subtle meat flavor, use only 2 cups cooked beans and add $\frac{1}{2}$ cup finely ground cooked chicken, pork or beef.

> $2\frac{1}{2}$ cups cooked beans (navy, limas, pinquitos or pinks), drained and mashed
> 1 egg, well beaten
> 1 whole onion, finely diced
> $\frac{1}{2}$ teaspoon salt
> $\frac{1}{2}$ teaspoon chili powder
> $\frac{1}{2}$ teaspoon freshly ground black pepper
> 1 small ground red chili (optional)
> Sufficient flour for coating
> Oil (preferably peanut) for frying
> Dijon mustard for dipping

Toss the first seven ingredients together and shape into walnut-sized balls. Roll in flour to coat. Heat oil to 360 degrees F, and sauté balls until crisp and brown. Drain on paper towel. Spear with toothpicks and serve with a French Dijon mustard as a dipping sauce.

Makes 20 to 25 balls.

Party Paté

Paté is always popular for parties. Serve this one hot or cold, to spread on small rounds of pumpernickel bread or garlic toast.

> 3 cups cooked cannellini or white kidney beans, drained
> 1 bunch scallions, chopped
> 2 cups grated carrots
> 3 tablespoons parsley, chopped
> 3 garlic cloves, mashed
> 2 tablespoons butter or margarine
> 2 eggs
> 1/2 cup cracker crumbs
> 1/2 cup half & half
> 1/2 teaspoon *each* salt, dry basil and thyme
> 1/4 cup dry Sherry

Put beans and scallions in food processor and grind to a fine meal. In a small pan, sauté carrots, parsley and garlic in butter or margarine until soft. Combine all ingredients in a large bowl and mix well. Butter an 8-inch baking dish and spoon in mixture, spreading evenly. Double a piece of waxed paper and cut to fit the baking dish. Butter the paper and place butter-side down on the mixture.

Bake at 400 degrees F for 50 to 55 minutes.

Makes an 8-inch round dish.

South American Popcorn

Popping beans—the colorful high-protein nuñas from the Andes—are imported from Bolivia, Ecuador and Peru into the United States. Nuñas expand when heated in hot oil, a popcorn popper or microwave. After toasting, they have a chewy texture with a peanut-like flavor. Present supplies of nuñas are small, and they may be hard to find, but you can generally track them down at South American groceries in some areas. The USDA's Agricultural Research Service is conducting experiments to grow them at high altitude in Colorado. When these domestically grown popping beans are produced, greater quantities will reach the markets.

$\frac{1}{2}$ lb nuñas (popping beans)
Peanut or vegetable oil for frying
Butter, salt, pepper or onion salt to taste

In a deep 10-inch covered skillet or large heavy pan, pour about 1 inch oil. Heat over medium-high heat. Make a single layer of nuña beans in the bottom of pan, being careful to keep the beans covered with oil or they will become hard and won't pop. Shake pan gently during cooking until popping sounds stop. Remove beans with a slotted spoon and blot well with several layers of paper towels. Place beans in serving bowl and sprinkle with butter and seasonings.

Makes 2 to 3 cups.

Swedish Mushroom Caps

Shop for mushrooms that are firm, white and large—the bigger the better.

12 large (2" to 3") mushrooms
$\frac{1}{2}$ cup cooked Swedish Brown beans, drained and
    mashed
$\frac{1}{2}$ cup fine bread crumbs
3 tablespoons fresh parsley, chopped
2 teaspoons dried oregano
$\frac{1}{2}$ medium onion, finely diced or minced
1 rib celery, finely diced
2 garlic cloves, mashed
2 oz ($\frac{1}{2}$ stick) butter or margarine
Parsley and red radishes for garnish

Wash and clean mushrooms and blot dry. Carefully remove stems and chop finely. Put the mushroom stems, beans, bread crumbs, parsley and oregano in a bowl. Sauté onion, celery and garlic in butter or margarine in a small pan, then add to bowl mixture and stir together. If too dry, moisten with a little more melted butter or margarine. Mound mixture on top of mushrooms.

Bake at 350 degrees F for about 20 minutes. Serve warm, garnished with parsley and radishes.

Makes 12 appetizers.

Vegetable Pizza

This is pizza with a difference. Served cold with a tangy, creamy topping, beans and vegetables, it has a refreshing taste. Make the crust a day ahead, cover with cellophane wrap and refrigerate. Assemble the topping on the pizza an hour before serving, otherwise the crust may become soggy.

> 2 (8-oz) tubes crescent dinner rolls
> Sour-cream topping (recipe below)
> Bean topping (recipe below)

Pat crescent roll dough into a 15″ x 10″ jelly roll pan and let stand 5 minutes. Pierce all over with a fork. Bake at 350 degrees F for 10 minutes, or till slightly golden brown, then cool. When ready to assemble, mix sour-cream topping ingredients together and spread generously on the cooled crust. Press beans and vegetables onto topping. Cover and chill for 1 hour, then cut into neat squares.

Sour-cream topping
> 1 cup *each* sour cream and mayonnaise
> 1 teaspoon *each* salt, garlic powder, onion powder, and
>   dried dill weed
> 1½ tablespoons dried parsley flakes
> 2 good twists of freshly ground pepper

Bean-and-vegetable topping
> 1 cup cooked Appaloosa beans, drained and cooled
> 1 cup *each* chopped cauliflower and chopped broccoli
> ½ cup *each* sliced red radishes, shredded carrots,
>   chopped celery and sliced red onion

Makes about 35 2-inch square appetizers.

Soups

Whether it be peasant-style beans and chunky vegetables for a hearty dinner in one bowl, or an elegant cream smoothed to velvety perfection, soups and beans are perfect company, to suit your mood or the moment.

  These soups will inspire you to further express your own creativity, tossing a handful of leftover beans in a rich broth to boost protein, serving them with different breads or crackers, and changing garnishes. Most soups freeze well, and can be made in advance to fit in with your busy week.

African Peanut Soup
Bean, Barley and Mushroom Soup
Black Bean Soup
Crowder Chowder
Danish Split Pea Soup
Gazpacho Olé!
The Great Garbanzo Soup
Magyar Soup
Minestrone Magnifico
Mung Bean Chowder
Sopa de Frijoles
Soup of Many Beans
Spectacular Spinach Soup
Zuppa di Verdura

African Peanut Soup

This sweet, rich and spicy soup was inspired by West African cuisine, and is for all peanut lovers.

> 1 cup onions, chopped
> 1 tablespoon oil
> 1 cup carrots, chopped
> $\frac{1}{2}$ to 1 teaspoon cayenne pepper
> 1 tablespoon sugar
> 1 teaspoon ginger root, grated
> 1 cup cooked peanut beans, drained
> 1 to $1\frac{1}{2}$ cups sweet potatoes or yams, chopped
> 4 cups vegetable stock (or 5 vegetarian bouillon cubes
>   dissolved in 4 cups water)
> 2 cups tomato juice
> 1 cup smooth peanut butter

In a large soup pot, sauté onions in oil till translucent. Add carrots, cayenne, sugar and ginger, and sauté a few more minutes. Add beans, potatoes and stock or water, and simmer till vegetables are tender. Purée the beans and vegetables in a food processor. Return to soup pot. Add tomato juice and stir in peanut butter till very smooth. If soup is too thick, thin with more stock or water. Reheat, stirring constantly till the desired consistency is reached.

Makes 6 to 8 servings.

Bean, Barley and Mushroom Soup

This hearty soup is a great favorite of ours. It's ethnic (Jewish) cooking from the Midwest—keeping the cold out, and tummy-satisfying. Served with French or sourdough bread and a fresh salad, it makes a complete dinner.

> 1 cup dried lima beans, soaked overnight, rinsed and drained
> 4 tablespoons pearl barley, soaked and drained
> 2 large onions, chopped
> 2 ribs celery, chopped
> 1 medium carrot, chopped
> 2 tablespoons fresh parsley, chopped
> 8 cups water
> $\frac{1}{2}$ lb fresh mushrooms, sliced
> $1\frac{1}{2}$ teaspoons salt, or to taste
> $\frac{1}{2}$ teaspoon freshly ground black pepper, or to taste

In a large soup pot, combine beans, barley, onions, celery, carrot, parsley and water. Cover and cook over low heat for about $2\frac{1}{2}$ hours or until beans are tender. Add mushrooms, salt and pepper. Cook for 10 minutes. Correct seasoning.

Makes 5 to 6 servings.

Black Bean Soup

A favorite soup in the West Indies. If you love foods searingly hot and spicy, garnish island-style with jalapeño peppers; or for a mild touch, decorate with parsley sprigs.

> 2 cups dried black beans, soaked and drained
> 8 cups cold water
> 3 tablespoons butter or margarine
> 2 ribs celery, chopped
> 1 large onion, chopped
> 2 garlic cloves, mashed
> 1 tablespoon flour
> 1/4 cup parsley, chopped
> 2 teaspoons liquid smoke seasoning
> 2 dried bay leaves
> 1 teaspoon cumin powder
> 1/2 cup dry Sherry or Madeira wine
> 2 tablespoons white vinegar
> Salt and freshly ground black pepper to taste
> 1 cup sour cream
> Jalapeño peppers or parsley sprigs for garnish

Place beans in a large soup pot with the cold water. Cover and simmer for 1 hour, then remove from stove.

In sauté pan, melt butter or margarine and sauté celery, onions and garlic till onions are translucent. Blend in flour, stirring for 1 minute.

Add onion mixture to beans, and add parsley, liquid smoke, bay leaves and cumin. Cover; simmer for 3 hours.

Remove bay leaves. Pour the soup into a food processor and purée with Sherry or wine, vinegar, salt and pepper. Return soup to pot, stir in sour cream and reheat thoroughly without letting it boil. Pour into soup bowls and garnish each serving with a jalapeño pepper or parsley sprig.

Makes 10 to 12 servings.

Crowder Chowder

No clams or corn in this special chowder. It's a tasty variation of an old favorite. The already-cooked crowder peas cut preparation time when you have to put supper on the table in a hurry.

> 1 small onion, diced
> 6 tablespoons butter or margarine
> 2 cups cooked crowder peas, drained
> 4 cups cooked potatoes, skinned and cubed
> 4 cups low-fat milk
> Salt and freshly ground pepper to taste

In a large soup pot, sauté onion in 3 tablespoons butter or margarine until translucent. Add all other ingredients and remainder of butter. Simmer till flavors blend.

Makes 6 to 8 servings.

Danish Split Pea Soup

Almost every continent and culture uses split peas in fanciful and flavorful ways. In Denmark, the national soup is probably split pea. Danes serve the soup along with pickled beets, a hearty rye bread, fresh unsalted butter, a good sharp mustard, beer and ice-cold *schnapps*.

In eighteenth century Prussia, pea soup was one of King Frederick the Great's favorites. It is still associated with the country's long military tradition and is a staple of the military menu. A number of sporting clubs in Germany continue to rent Army field kitchens for providing refreshment at members' meetings, and cook up enormous batches of split pea soup.

$2\frac{1}{4}$ cups dried yellow split peas
5 cups water
$1\frac{3}{4}$ cups vegetable stock
1 large leek, thinly sliced
1 medium carrot, thinly sliced
2 large garlic cloves, peeled and halved
$\frac{1}{2}$ teaspoon dried thyme leaves, crumbled
$\frac{1}{2}$ teaspoon white pepper
$\frac{3}{4}$ teaspoon salt, or to taste

Put all ingredients except salt into a heavy 4-quart pot. Cover and bring to a boil over high heat. Reduce heat and simmer gently for about $1\frac{1}{2}$ hours, stirring occasionally, until peas are sufficiently tender to make a purée. Remove from heat and stir in salt.

Note: For Caribbean-style soup, use green split peas instead of yellow, and season with 1 teaspoon ground cumin instead of thyme.

Makes 8 one-cup servings.

Gazpacho Olé!

The flavor of Spain! A cold soup that's just as good in winter as it is in summer.

4 medium size tomatoes, chopped
1 medium green bell pepper, seeded and chopped
1 large cucumber, chopped
4 scallions, chopped
2 garlic cloves, mashed
2 small sprigs fresh parsley, chopped
3 cups tomato juice
$\frac{1}{2}$ cup cooked pigeon peas, drained and cooled
$\frac{1}{4}$ cup *each* red-wine vinegar and olive oil
Salt and freshly ground black pepper to taste
Garnishes: thin lime slices, chopped hard-cooked eggs,
          croutons, scallions

Place the tomatoes, cucumber, bell pepper, scallions, garlic and parsley in a food processor. Process to small pieces. In a large bowl add vegetables to tomato juice, pigeon peas, vinegar and oil. Add salt and ground pepper. Chill and serve with garnishes.

Makes 2 quarts or about 8 servings.

The Great Garbanzo Soup

Cumin, cayenne and cilantro bring a zesty Latin flavor to this soup, and the buttermilk adds a smooth velvety texture.

    1 bunch scallions, chopped
    2 garlic cloves, mashed
    2 teaspoons fresh parsley, chopped
    1 tablespoon olive oil
    1 cup cooked garbanzos (chickpeas), drained
    4 large carrots, thinly sliced
    4 cups water
    1 teaspoon ground cumin
    $\frac{1}{4}$ teaspoon cayenne pepper
    1 cup buttermilk
    1 tablespoon *each* dried mint, chopped cilantro and
        lemon juice

In a soup pot, sauté scallions, garlic and parsley in olive oil for 5 minutes. Stir in garbanzos, carrots, water and spices. Bring to a boil and simmer 35 minutes. Remove from heat.

Put soup in food processor and process till smooth. Return soup to the pot and stir in buttermilk, mint, cilantro and lemon juice. Stir over low heat till hot, but not boiling.

Makes 4 to 6 servings.

Magyar Bean Soup

Magyar is Hungarian style, and Hungarians are renowned for being outstanding cooks.

The city of Szeged in southeast Hungary is one of the centers for growing paprika and this ingredient finds its way into many typical dishes of the region. Paprika can be sweet or hot, and it is the Szeged *sweet* variety that gives this soup an authentic and distinctive touch. This special paprika is imported into the United States and can be found in most supermarkets.

> 2 large leeks, cleaned and chopped
> 1 carrot, diced
> 2 garlic cloves, mashed
> 3 tablespoons chopped fresh parsley (or 1 tablespoon dried)
> 2 tablespoons oil
> 3 tablespoons flour
> 2 teaspoons Szeged sweet paprika
> 1/4 teaspoon freshly ground black pepper
> 2 cups water
> 1 cup cooked baby lima beans, drained
> 1/4 cup sour cream
> 2 tablespoons lemon juice

In a soup pot, sauté leeks, carrot, garlic and parsley in oil for 10 minutes. Mix in flour, paprika and pepper; cook 5 more minutes. Add water, stirring till smooth and thickened. Stir in the beans and cook 10 minutes over low heat.

Remove soup from the stove and add sour cream and lemon juice. Reheat for another 10 minutes, without letting soup boil, stirring constantly.

Makes 4 servings.

Minestrone Magnifico

A culinary treasure typical of the cuisine of Italy. This one from the Tuscany region can adapt to any season depending on the vegetables used. Serve with Italian bread, garlic toast or breadsticks and a green salad. For hearty appetites, you might like to add a side dish of Italian-style corn polenta.

$\frac{1}{2}$ lb dried cranberry beans, soaked and drained
$\frac{1}{2}$ lb dried cannellini beans, soaked and drained
3 quarts vegetable stock (or 5 vegetarian bouillon cubes
        dissolved in 3 quarts water)
2 garlic cloves, mashed
1 bay leaf
2 tablespoons fresh parsley, chopped
$\frac{1}{2}$ cup tomato sauce
2 medium carrots, diced
2 medium-size red potatoes, diced
$\frac{1}{2}$ green cabbage, shredded
1 large onion, chopped
$\frac{1}{2}$ lb fresh mushrooms, sliced
$\frac{1}{2}$ cup peas, fresh or frozen
2 medium zucchini, sliced
$\frac{1}{2}$ teaspoon *each* dried basil and thyme
1 cup uncooked macaroni
Salt and freshly ground black pepper to taste
Freshly grated Parmesan cheese

Cook beans, stock, garlic, bay leaf and parsley. Cover and bring to the boil. Let simmer until beans are cooked. Add tomato sauce, vegetables, basil and thyme, and simmer about 1 hour until vegetables are cooked. Remove bay leaf and add macaroni 10 minutes before serving. Simmer till macaroni is tender. Add salt and pepper. Ladle into soup bowls. Place cheese in a separate bowl to pass around for topping.

Makes 6 to 8 servings.

Mung Bean Chowder

This chowder needs no pre-soaking or pre-cooking and is prepared in only 30 minutes. A very thick soup that's filling and satisfying. You can buy rice grits and tamari in health-food stores.

$1/2$ cup mung beans
$1/2$ cup short grain brown rice or rice grits
$1/4$ cup sesame seeds
1 tablespoon dried onion flakes
2 teaspoons parsley flakes
1 teaspoon *each* dried dill weed and ground fennel
$1/2$ teaspoon garlic powder
$1/2$ teaspoon ground cumin
2 teaspoons tamari sauce or soy sauce
$3^1/_2$ cups water

Mix all the dry ingredients with the water. Bring to a boil, and cook on medium to low heat for about 30 minutes, stirring occasionally.

Makes 4 servings.

Sopa Frijoles

The Tarascan Indians who live in the highlands of Michoacan State in Mexico are known for their hearty soups made with beans, chilis and tomatoes. This soup thickens considerably as it cooks and may be diluted with more broth or water.

$\frac{1}{2}$ medium onion, sliced
2 garlic cloves, mashed
2 large tomatoes, chopped
$\frac{1}{2}$ lb dried Tongues of Fire beans, cooked and drained
6 cups vegetable stock (or 8 vegetarian bouillon cubes
      dissolved in 6 cups water)
Salt and freshly ground black pepper to taste
$\frac{1}{2}$ lb Monterey Jack cheese, finely diced
3 small green chilis
1 cup tortilla chips, broken into quarters
Sour cream (optional)

In a food processor, whirl onion, garlic and tomatoes to fine pieces. Cook for about 5 minutes. Process beans and 3 cups of vegetable stock to make a purée. Pour purée in a soup pot, add tomato mixture and cook for 10 minutes over medium heat, stirring constantly. Add the other 3 cups of stock and cook another 10 minutes. Season with salt and pepper. Divide cheese into 6 bowls. Pour soup over cheese, add chilis and tortilla chips. Finish with a dollop of sour cream, if desired.

Makes 6 servings.

The Soup of Many Beans

(Joseph's Soup)

Five different kinds of dried legumes make up this pretty soup.
Serve with a side dish of rice or pasta and a green salad, and you
have a complete meal. The sun-dried tomatoes add a splash of
color; they can be found in most large supermarkets in the
specialty produce section.

$\frac{1}{4}$ lb dried white kidney beans, soaked and rinsed
$\frac{1}{2}$ lb dried fava beans, soaked and rinsed
$\frac{1}{4}$ lb dried garbanzos (chickpeas)
$\frac{1}{4}$ lb dried lentils, any color
$\frac{1}{4}$ lb dried split yellow peas
9 to 10 cups water
1 (5-oz) can water chestnuts, drained and sliced
3 ribs celery, chopped
1 medium onion, diced
1 medium carrot, chopped
6 sun-dried tomatoes, chopped small
2 garlic cloves, mashed
3 teaspoons ground fennel seeds
Salt and freshly ground black pepper to taste
Seasoned croutons

Drain legumes, rinse and put into soup pot with water.
Bring to a boil and simmer for about 3 hours, until all
legumes are tender. Half-way through cooking ($1\frac{1}{2}$
hours), add water chestnuts, celery, onion, carrot,
tomatoes, garlic and fennel. When cooked, correct seasoning. Ladle soup into bowls, top with seasoned croutons and serve.

Makes 6 to 8 servings.

Spectacular Spinach Soup

A refreshing soup to be served cold in summertime. Elegant and simple, this one cooks in 15 minutes.

1 cup cooked Jackson Wonder beans, drained
1 (10-oz) package frozen spinach, thawed and chopped
2 cups water
1 tablespoon sugar
$1/4$ teaspoon salt
Juice of 1 lemon
Sour cream

Mix all ingredients except sour cream in a soup pot. Bring to a boil and simmer for 15 minutes. Chill and serve cold with a dollop of sour cream.

Makes 2 to 4 servings.

Zuppa di Verdura

Similar to a minestrone or vegetable soup, but the addition of Swiss chard creates a lovely new fresh flavor.

> 1 medium onion, chopped
> 2 ribs celery, chopped
> 1 carrot, chopped
> 2 garlic cloves, mashed
> $\frac{1}{2}$ cup fresh parsley, chopped
> $\frac{1}{3}$ cup olive oil
> 1 lb baccicia beans, soaked overnight, rinsed and drained
> 6 cups hot water
> 1 lb fresh Swiss chard, washed and cut into $\frac{1}{2}$-inch pieces
> Salt and freshly ground black pepper to taste
> 6 slices Italian bread, toasted

Sauté onion, celery, carrot, garlic and parsley in olive oil for 5 minutes. Add beans and water to the vegetables and simmer 1 hour or until beans are almost tender.

Add Swiss chard and cook 10 more minutes until chard is tender. Season to taste. Place one piece of toasted bread in each soup bowl. Spoon soup onto toast and serve.

Makes 6 servings.

Salads

An attractive bean salad should have the beans cooked until just tender to keep skins intact, and thoroughly drained. Unless the salad is intended to be served warm, it's best to cool the beans, uncovered, and chill before tossing in dressing, marinade or other ingredients.

Adzuki Oriental Salad
Anasazi Aspic
Appaloosa Wagon Wheels
Attention! Salad
Christmas Lima Combo
Cranberry Orange Tangy Salad
Cuban-Style Bean Salad
Da Beanie Tabbouleh
Domino Salad
Indian Wonder Salad
Layered Four Bean Salad
Lotsa Lentils Salad
Molded Bean Salad
Potato and Peanut Bean Salad
Romano Flageolet Salad
Runner Bean Roundup

Adzuki Oriental Salad

Most adzuki beans are imported from Japan, where for years they were used as a remedy for kidney problems. Like all beans, these richly colored delights are a good source of protein, vitamins and minerals.

This salad is versatile because the character can be changed from Oriental to Italian by using a creamy Italian dressing and topping with freshly grated Parmesan cheese.

>   1 cup cooked adzuki beans, drained
>   3 cups cooked pasta (small shells, spirals or elbow
>   macaroni)
>   1 scallion, minced
>   1/4 cup fresh parsley, minced
>   2 ribs celery, diced
>   1/2 green bell pepper, seeded and diced
>   1 medium carrot, grated
>   Oriental dressing (see recipe below)

Mix salad ingredients together and toss with Oriental dressing. Serve well chilled.

Oriental dressing
>   1/4 cup walnuts, finely chopped
>   2 tablespoons sugar
>   6 tablespoons rice vinegar
>   4 tablespoons soy sauce
>   2 tablespoons sesame oil

Mix together and toss over salad.

Makes 4 to 6 servings.

Anasazi Aspic

This salad is made with canned aspic that can be found in most supermarkets. Seasoning the Anasazi beans with garlic and onion gives them great flavor.

1 lb Anasazi beans, cooked, drained and chilled
1 tablespoon garlic powder
1 tablespoon onion powder
1 (13½-oz) can tomato aspic, chilled
2 cups low-fat cottage cheese
Lemon wedges for garnish

In a small bowl, mix garlic and onion powders with the chilled beans. Cut the chilled aspic into thick slices and arrange on a serving platter. Spoon beans onto aspic, and surround with mounds of cottage cheese. Garnish with lemon wedges and serve.

Makes 4 to 6 servings.

Appaloosa Wagon Wheels

Imagine sitting around a campfire in the Old West, with the beans and corn cooking in the pot. This salad goes well with any grilled foods at summertime outdoor barbecues.

1 cup cooked Appaloosa beans, drained
1 cup cooked wagon-wheel pasta (or small elbow
    macaroni), drained
1 cup canned whole-kernel corn, drained
$\frac{1}{4}$ cup fresh parsley, chopped
$\frac{1}{3}$ cup olive oil
$\frac{1}{4}$ cup cider vinegar
2 tablespoons Dijon mustard
2 garlic cloves, minced
1 teaspoon *each* ground cumin and chili powder
1 teaspoon cayenne pepper (optional)

Mix beans, pasta, corn and parsley in a medium bowl. In a smaller bowl, blend oil, vinegar, mustard, garlic, cumin, chili powder and cayenne pepper. Toss together with bean and pasta mixture. Serve at room temperature.

Makes 4 to 6 servings.

(Adapted from a recipe provided by Good Taste of Ketchum, Idaho, and reproduced with their kind permission.)

Attention! Salad

Look closely at the markings on European Soldier beans and you'll see a soldier standing to *attention!* This salad uses these distinctively marked beans with their special coloring and good flavor.

Basmati rice (named after the city of Basmat in the State of Maharashtra in Central India) is noted for its intensely fragrant aroma and the extraordinary length of its cooked grains. Some of the best Basmati is imported from India, and can be bought in specialty grocery stores here. Many chefs recognize Basmati's ability to transform rice dishes into outstanding concoctions, and prefer to cook with no other kind.

> 1 cup cooked European Soldier beans, drained
> 1 cup cooked Basmati or long-grain rice, drained
> 1 carrot, thinly sliced
> $\frac{1}{2}$ cup mushrooms, thinly sliced
> $\frac{1}{2}$ cup zucchini, thinly sliced
> $\frac{1}{4}$ cup fresh parsley, finely chopped
> 1 garlic clove, minced
> $\frac{1}{2}$ cup olive oil
> $\frac{1}{3}$ cup white wine vinegar
> 1 teaspoon ground cinnamon
> $\frac{1}{2}$ teaspoon ground cumin
> Salt and freshly ground black pepper to taste

In a medium bowl, mix beans, rice, carrot, mushrooms, zucchini, parsley and garlic. In a smaller bowl, blend together the oil, vinegar, cinnamon, cumin, salt and pepper, then gently toss the dressing with the bean mixture. Serve at room temperature.

Makes 4 to 6 servings.

Christmas Lima Combo

A potato salad with a difference. This one has a sweet-sour taste that's great for picnics and buffet tables.

4 cups cooked potatoes, unpeeled, drained, cooled and diced
1 cup cooked Christmas limas, drained and cooled
1 medium red onion, sliced
$\frac{1}{2}$ cup celery, chopped
$\frac{1}{3}$ cup sugar
$\frac{1}{3}$ cup cider vinegar
$\frac{1}{2}$ teaspoon dry mustard
Imitation bacon bits

In a medium bowl, mix potatoes, beans, onion and celery. In a smaller bowl, blend sugar, vinegar and mustard, then add to potato-bean mixture. Sprinkle with imitation bacon bits. Serve warm or at room temperature.

Makes 4 to 6 servings.

(Adapted from a recipe provided by Good Taste of Ketchum, Idaho, and reproduced with their kind permission.)

Cranberry Orange Tangy Salad

Mandarin oranges and cranberry sauce make this salad colorful and very refreshing, giving the beans a special tang.

1 cup cooked cranberry beans, drained and chilled
$\frac{1}{2}$ cup chopped walnuts
1 medium red onion, chopped
7 tablespoons oil
3 tablespoons balsamic or malt vinegar
6 tablespoons canned whole-berry cranberry sauce
1 small can mandarin oranges

In a medium bowl, mix drained beans with walnuts and onion. In a smaller bowl, blend the oil, vinegar and cranberry sauce. Toss with the bean mixture. Serve chilled on a bed of salad greens, topped with the mandarin oranges.

Makes 4 to 6 servings.

(Adapted from a recipe provided by Good Taste of Ketchum, Idaho, and reproduced with their kind permission.)

Cuban-Style Bean Salad

Try these vinegar-with-oil beans in place of the usual baked beans at your next cookout or barbecue.

1 medium onion, chopped
1 medium green bell pepper, seeded and chopped
1 medium red bell pepper, seeded and chopped
2 garlic cloves, mashed
5 tablespoons olive oil
1 teaspoon ground cumin
1 bay leaf
1 cup tomato sauce
2 tablespoons *each* vinegar and red wine
1 lb yellow-eye beans, cooked, drained and chilled

Brown onion, bell peppers and garlic in 3 tablespoons of the olive oil. Add cumin and bay leaf and cook for 5 minutes till onion is translucent. Add tomato sauce and cook 5 more minutes. Remove bay leaf and put tomato mixture in a food processor or blender and whirl until smooth. Add vinegar, wine and remaining oil. Add to cooked, cooled beans. Serve.

Makes 6 to 8 servings.

Da Beanie Tabbouleh

Tabbouleh is a Middle East favorite. This Jordanian version, made light and refreshing with mint and lemon, is one that perfectly complements almost any summertime meal.

Bulgur wheat can be found at Middle Eastern/Mediterranean shops, health-food stores and some supermarkets. Check packages, as some bulgur is pre-cooked and needs no soaking before use.

> 1 cup bulgur wheat
> $3^3/_4$ cups boiling water
> 1 cup cooked fava beans, drained and cooled
> 1 large cucumber, seeded and diced
> $1/_2$ cup scallions, thinly sliced
> $1/_2$ cup olive oil
> $1/_2$ cup lemon juice
> 1 tablespoon fresh mint leaves, chopped
>   (or $1/_2$ tablespoon dried)
> 2 garlic cloves, minced
> Salt and freshly ground pepper to taste
> 1 large tomato, chopped
> Mint sprigs for garnish

In a large bowl, pour boiling water over the bulgur wheat. Cover and let stand until light and fluffy—about 2 hours. Shake in a colander and squeeze out any excess water.

Mix drained bulgur, beans, cucumber and scallions and set aside. In a smaller bowl, blend olive oil, lemon juice, chopped mint and garlic, and add to bean-bulgur mixture. Chill at least 1 hour. Longer chilling brings out the mint flavor. Before serving, add chopped tomato and garnish with mint sprigs.

Makes 6 to 8 servings.

Domino Salad

White beans and dark rice create the domino effect in this cool, appealing salad that's just right for a hot afternoon.

> 1 lb cannellini beans, cooked, drained and chilled
> 2 cups cooked wild rice, chilled
> 1 cup mayonnaise
> 2 tablespoons Dijon mustard
> 1 teaspoon Worcestershire sauce
> Salt and freshly ground black pepper to taste
> 2 teaspoons milk, if needed to thin dressing
> Salad greens
> 2 tomatoes, cut in wedges
> 2 hard-cooked eggs, cut in wedges
> 1 medium green bell pepper, seeded, cut in strips

In a medium bowl, mix beans and rice. In a smaller bowl, blend mayonnaise, mustard, Worcestershire sauce, salt and pepper and milk, if needed. Gently toss with rice and beans. Arrange salad greens on 4 plates and mound rice-bean mixture in center of each plate. Arrange tomato, eggs and bell pepper around each plate edge. Chill and serve.

Makes 4 servings.

Indian Wonder Salad

Curry, raisins and walnuts give the beans a marvelous flavor, dressed with cool yogurt.

> 2 cups cooked Jackson Wonder beans, drained and
>   cooled
> 2 cups cooked Basmati or long-grain rice, cooled
> 1 medium green bell pepper, seeded and cut in strips
> 2 tablespoons pimientos, drained, cut in strips
> 1/3 cup golden raisins
> 1/3 cup walnuts, chopped
> 1/4 cup scallions, finely chopped
> 1 cup plain nonfat yogurt
> 1 tablespoon lemon juice
> 1 garlic clove, mashed
> 2 tablespoons sugar
> 3 teaspoons curry powder
> Salt and freshly ground black pepper to taste

In a medium bowl, mix beans, rice, bell pepper, pimientos, raisins, walnuts and scallions. In a smaller bowl, blend yogurt with lemon juice, garlic, sugar, curry powder, salt and pepper. Toss with bean and rice mixture. Serve.

Makes 4 to 6 servings.

Layered Four Bean Salad

When looking for a salad to serve a crowd, this is the one. The layers use four different kinds and colors of beans to make a brilliant and impressive presentation at the dining table.

$1/2$ cup *each* sugar, red-wine vinegar and salad oil
2 tablespoons fresh parsley, chopped
$1/2$ teaspoon dry mustard
2 teaspoons fresh basil, or $3/4$ teaspoon dried
$1/2$ teaspoon oregano
Salt and freshly ground black pepper to taste
Romaine lettuce leaves
1 lb Black Valentine beans, cooked, drained and chilled
1 lb French navy beans, cooked, drained and chilled
1 lb jumbo pinto runner beans, cooked, drained and chilled
1 lb Christmas lima beans, cooked, drained and chilled
1 medium red onion, sliced and separated into rings

In a small bowl, mix sugar, vinegar, oil, parsley, mustard, basil, oregano, salt and pepper; set aside.

Line a large glass bowl with romaine lettuce leaves. Layer the Black Valentine beans in the bowl and drizzle with about a quarter of the oil-vinegar dressing. Add the French navy beans and drizzle with more dressing. Continue until you have four layers. Garnish top with red onion rings, then chill thoroughly.

Makes 12 generous servings.

Lotsa Lentils Salad

The two colors of lentils make this salad really attractive, and since lentils cook in about 10 to 15 minutes, you can quickly put this one together.

$\frac{1}{2}$ cup mild onion, finely chopped
$\frac{1}{2}$ cup commercial mild salsa
2 teaspoons chili powder
$\frac{1}{2}$ teaspoon dried oregano
2 tablespoons lemon juice
1 cup fresh spinach, chopped
$\frac{1}{2}$ cup cooked Turkish red lentils, drained and chilled
$\frac{1}{2}$ cup cooked yellow lentils, drained and chilled
Whole spinach leaves for arrangement

In a small bowl, blend onion, salsa, chili powder, oregano and lemon juice, and set aside. Put chopped spinach in a medium bowl and toss in the salsa mixture, then add the lentils. Line salad bowls with the whole spinach leaves and mound salad on top.

Makes 4 servings.

Molded Bean Salad

This salad is made with a plain gelatin so the beans and vegetables are flavorful and appealing.

  1 envelope unflavored gelatin
  $1/4$ cup sugar
  $1/2$ teaspoon *each* salt and freshly ground black pepper
  $1^1/2$ cups water
  2 tablespoons lemon juice
  $1/2$ cup cooked Steuben yellow-eye beans, drained and
      cooled
  $1/2$ cup carrots, finely chopped
  $1/2$ cup celery, finely chopped
  $1/2$ cup green bell pepper, seeded and finely chopped
  Red lettuce or spinach leaves

In a small pan, mix gelatin, sugar, salt and pepper. Add $1/2$ cup of water and heat gently until the gelatin dissolves thoroughly, stirring constantly. Remove from stove and add the remaining cup of water and lemon juice. Stir well and allow to cool slightly.

Combine beans and vegetables and fold into gelatin mixture. Pour into a 3-cup mold and chill thoroughly until firm, preferably overnight. Remove from mold and serve on a plate lined with red lettuce or spinach.

Makes 6 servings.

Potato and Peanut Bean Salad

Good ol' American potato salad with the addition of beans for taste and color. A great combination of two nutritious foods that is a family favorite.

4 cups cooked potatoes, chilled and cubed
1 cup cooked peanut beans, drained and chilled
2 hard-cooked eggs, chilled and chopped
$\frac{1}{2}$ cup celery, chopped
1 medium red onion, thinly sliced
$\frac{1}{4}$ cup sweet pickle relish, or chopped pickle
1 to $1\frac{1}{2}$ cups mayonnaise
2 teaspoons Worcestershire sauce
1 teaspoon Dijon mustard
$\frac{1}{2}$ teaspoon garlic powder
Salt and freshly ground black pepper to taste
Paprika and parsley garnish

In a large bowl, mix together potatoes, beans, eggs, celery, onion and relish or sweet pickle. In a smaller bowl, blend mayonnaise, Worcestershire sauce, mustard, garlic powder, salt and pepper. Add dressing to the potato-bean mixture. Sprinkle top with paprika and garnish with parsley sprigs.

Makes 6 to 8 servings.

Romano Flageolet Salad

Hot crusty French bread and a good bottle of wine make this a perfect luncheon meal.

> 1 lb green or white flageolet beans, cooked, drained and chilled
> 1/2 cup black olives, sliced
> 1/2 cup canned artichoke hearts, drained
> 1/3 cup freshly grated Romano cheese
> 2 tablespoons pimiento, chopped
> 2 tablespoons capers
> 1 tablespoon fresh parsley, chopped
> 1/3 cup olive oil
> 1/3 cup white-wine vinegar
> 2 garlic cloves, finely minced
> 2 tablespoons fresh basil, chopped
> Salt and freshly ground pepper to taste

In a medium bowl, mix beans, olives, artichokes, cheese, pimiento, capers and parsley. In a smaller bowl, blend olive oil, vinegar, garlic, basil, salt and pepper. Pour over bean mixture. Chill and serve.

Makes 3 to 4 servings.

Runner Bean Roundup

An interesting and colorful fruit and bean combination, with the fruit bringing out the sweet nutty taste of the beans.

1 cup cooked scarlet runner or reverse scarlet runner
  beans, drained and chilled
$1/2$ cup blue cheese, crumbled
4 tablespoons white-wine vinegar
8 tablespoons olive oil
$1/4$ teaspoon freshly ground black pepper
$1/2$ cup chopped celery
$1/2$ cup chopped apple, unpeeled
Salad greens for garnish

In a small bowl, mix cheese, olive oil, vinegar and black pepper till creamy. Set aside. Place chilled beans in a medium bowl and stir in dressing. Add celery and apple. Chill and serve on a bed of salad greens.

Makes 4 to 6 servings.

Main Dishes

The protein in beans makes a good meat substitute when partnered with grains, cheeses or eggs. The beauty of legumes is that they go well with any seasoning. Use the seasonings listed here, but don't hesitate to be adventurous with your own favorite herbs and spices the next time around.

Barbecue Soy Burgers
Black Runner Frittata
Crepes à la Stroganoff
Hungarian Stew
Leek and Bean Quiche
Lentil Walnut Dogs
Mediterranean Eggplant and Garbanzos
Monday Night Chili
Pesto and Pasta
Shepherd's Pie
Soldier Croquettes with Mushroom Sauce
Spinach Soybean Soufflé
Vegetable Bean Lasagna

Barbecue Soy Burgers

These nutty-flavored burgers are a barbecue favorite, great on whole-wheat onion buns, with the traditional toppings of tomato, cheese, lettuce and so on.

   1 small onion, minced
   2 garlic cloves, mashed
   2 tablespoons butter or margarine
   2 cups cooked soybeans, drained
   $1/2$ cup fine bread crumbs
   1 egg
   2 tablespoons soy sauce
   2 tablespoons sesame seeds
   Freshly ground black pepper to taste

In a small pan, sauté onion and garlic in butter or margarine, and cook till translucent. Set aside.

In food processor, whirl beans, bread crumbs, egg, soy sauce and sesame seeds to a coarse meal. Transfer to a medium bowl, add onion-garlic mixture and black pepper, and mix well. Shape into four patties.

Heat on grill till brown, giving them about 5 minutes on each side.

Makes 4 burgers.

Black Runner Frittata

An easy supper dish that goes together quickly after you have had a hard day and the family is already asking "What's for dinner?"

 2 tablespoons vegetable oil
 3 cups cabbage, coarsely shredded
 1 medium onion, chopped
 1 garlic clove, mashed
 8 oz raw potatoes, shredded
 1 cup cooked black runner beans, well drained
 $\frac{1}{2}$ teaspoon fennel seeds
 2 eggs
 $\frac{1}{4}$ cup low-fat milk
 2 teaspoons Dijon mustard
 Salt and freshly ground black pepper to taste

In a large fry pan, heat 1 tablespoon vegetable oil over medium heat. Add cabbage, onion, and garlic, and cook for 5 minutes, stirring often. Add remaining tablespoon of oil and raw potatoes. Lower heat and cook for another 5 minutes until potatoes are cooked. Mix in beans and fennel.

 In a small bowl, beat eggs and blend in milk, mustard, salt and pepper. Pour over mixture in pan, tilting pan to distribute egg blend. Reduce heat, cover, and cook 5 minutes or until set. Run spatula around edge of pan to loosen frittata. Cut in wedges to serve.

Makes 4 servings.

Crepes à la Stroganoff

Crepes, or light French pancakes, can be prepared ahead of time and filled with a variety of foods. Beans are perfect in crepes because they blend so well with sauces and vegetables.

8 to 10 six-inch crepes (recipe below)
$\frac{1}{2}$ cup chopped onion
2 garlic cloves, mashed
2 tablespoons butter or margarine
$\frac{1}{2}$ lb Black Valentine beans, cooked and drained
$\frac{1}{2}$ lb fresh mushrooms, sliced
2 tablespoons Worcestershire sauce
$\frac{1}{2}$ cup dry red wine
1 cup sour cream

Make crepes then set aside and make filling.

Sauté onions and garlic in butter till onions are translucent. Add beans, mushrooms, Worcestershire sauce and wine. Simmer about 15 minutes, till well blended and wine has evaporated. Add $\frac{3}{4}$ cup of the sour cream and heat through gently.

To assemble: place a small spoonful of filling onto each crepe. Roll up and put in a buttered ovenproof serving dish, 7" x 12". When all crepes are ready, run the dish under the broiler 2 to 3 minutes to heat through. Garnish each crepe with a tiny dollop of remaining sour cream.

Basic crepe recipe (for 8 to 10 six-inch crepes)

1 cup low-fat milk
1 egg
1 cup all-purpose flour
1 tablespoon butter or margarine, melted

Place all ingredients in a blender for 30 to 40 seconds till cream-like. Spoon two or three tablespoons of batter into a well-greased crepe pan. Tilt pan so batter covers the bottom. Cook over medium heat. When crepe is set, crisp around edges and lightly browned, flip over to brown other side. Remove and stack on plate until ready to fill.

Makes 8 crepes or 4 servings.

Hungarian Stew

A stew with four legumes, well-flavored with turnips and carrots, and hearty for a cold winter evening beside a crackling log fire. Serve the stew piping hot with a warm, crusty baguette or French bread.

1 medium onion, chopped
2 garlic cloves, mashed
2 tablespoons vegetable oil
$1\frac{1}{2}$ teaspoons Szeged (Hungarian) sweet paprika
$\frac{1}{2}$ cup dried yellow split peas, soaked and drained
$\frac{1}{2}$ cup dried Anasazi beans, soaked and drained
$\frac{1}{2}$ cup dried cannellini beans, soaked and drained
$\frac{1}{2}$ cup dried Dixie butter peas, soaked and drained
1 bay leaf
6 cups water
$\frac{1}{2}$ cup turnips, diced
1 cup carrots, diced
$\frac{1}{2}$ cup celery, chopped
2 teaspoons salt
Freshly ground black pepper to taste

Sauté onion and garlic in oil with paprika. Add beans, bay leaf and water. Bring to boil. Simmer covered for 1 hour. Add vegetables, salt and pepper and simmer 1 more hour or until beans and vegetables are tender. Remove bay leaf and serve hot.

Makes 4 to 6 servings.

Leek and Bean Quiche

Served warm or cold, this quiche is perfect for a luncheon or light supper. It's also good served cold as an appetizer.

1 9-inch unbaked pie crust (recipe below)
1 cup leeks, washed and sliced
2 tablespoons butter or margarine
1 tablespoon all-purpose flour
$\frac{1}{2}$ lb Gruyère cheese (or mild Swiss), grated
2 tablespoons freshly grated Parmesan cheese
2 cups cooked Florida butter beans, drained
3 eggs
$1\frac{1}{2}$ cups half & half
Freshly ground black pepper to taste
2 medium tomatoes, thinly sliced

Make pie crust and set aside.

In a small pan, sauté leeks in butter or margarine till translucent. In a medium bowl, mix flour with grated cheeses, beans and cooked leeks. Spread cheese-leek mixture evenly across bottom of pastry-lined pie pan. Beat eggs, half & half and pepper together. Pour over mixture in pan.

Bake at 350 degrees F for 45 minutes to 1 hour, or until an inserted knife blade comes out clean. Allow to stand 15 minutes before serving. Garnish with tomato slices.

For *Quiche crust*, please turn page.

Quiche crust

> 4 oz (1 stick) margarine
> 1¼ cups all-purpose flour
> Sprinkle of salt
> 2 tablespoons *ice*-cold water

Mix all ingredients till ball forms. Chill for about 1 hour. Roll out on floured board and place in a quiche pan or 9-inch pie pan.

Makes 1 9-inch quiche, about 6 luncheon-size servings.

Lentil Walnut Dogs

Serve these "hot-dogs" on French bread, spread with honey mustard, and lavished with grilled onions. Delicious!

> 2 cups cooked lentils
> ½ cup chopped walnuts
> 2 scallions, minced
> 1 egg, beaten
> 3 tablespoons fine bread crumbs
> ¼ cup soy sauce
> 1 teaspoon dried thyme

In a food processor, process lentils to a coarse meal. In a medium bowl, combine all other ingredients and add lentils. Mix well. Shape into 4 oblong patties and flatten slightly. Broil or grill on the barbecue, about 4 minutes on each side.

Makes 4 2"x 5" "hot-dogs."

Mediterranean Eggplant and Garbanzos

Garbanzos and eggplant always blend perfectly in Middle Eastern cuisine, and this dish is no exception. If you have an electric fry pan, preparation is beautifully simple.

1 large eggplant
2 medium onions, sliced
2 garlic cloves, mashed
1 large red bell pepper, seeded and sliced
2 tablespoons olive oil
2 medium zucchini, sliced
2 cups cooked garbanzos, drained
2 medium tomatoes, cut into eighths
1 can (16-oz) tomatoes, drained and chopped
$1/2$ teaspoon *each* dried turmeric, oregano and thyme
1 teaspoon ground cinnamon

Prick eggplant skin in several places with a fork and place on paper towel in microwave oven. Pre-cook in microwave on full power for 10 minutes. Cool, slice thickly and set aside.

In fry pan, sauté onions, garlic and bell pepper in olive oil till soft. Add eggplant, zucchini, beans, tomatoes, canned tomatoes and spices. Cook until well-blended and eggplant and zucchini are soft. If using electric fry pan, cook on 300 degrees F for about $1/2$ hour; if using regular pan, cook on low heat for about 40 minutes.

Makes 6 servings.

Monday Night Chili

An easy dish when you want a simple supper for your "armchair athletes" or a few close friends. The canned refried beans make a quick thickener. The chili seasoning is mild and the garlic understated; garlic lovers can toss in a few more spikes to increase the voltage. Serve with warm cornbread (homemade or a mix) or good crusty Italian bread, and a big bowl of freshly tossed salad greens.

    1 tablespoon canola oil
    1 large onion, chopped
    2 ribs celery, chopped
    3 garlic cloves, peeled and minced
    1 medium red or green bell pepper, seeded and
        chopped
    1 lb red beans (preferably Santa Maria), soaked, cooked
        and drained
    1 (15-oz) can kidney beans, drained and rinsed
    1 (28-oz) can crushed tomatoes, with can liquid
    1 (15-oz) can refried bean
    1 tablespoon chili powder
    1 tablespoon cumin
    Salt and pepper to taste
    1 cup Jack cheese, shredded (optional)

Heat oil in large fry pan then sauté onion, celery, garlic and bell pepper until onion is translucent. Add cooked red beans, canned kidney beans and crushed tomatoes. Cook 30 minutes. Add canned refried beans and seasonings, and simmer for another 30 minutes. Top each bowl with a sprinkling of cheese, if you like.

Makes 6 to 8 servings.

Pesto and Pasta

Pesto makes a good alternative to marinara sauce—very simple, no long cooking involved, and it's ready to serve in minutes. Ladle the sauce atop hot spaghetti, and serve with warm crusty French bread, a fresh crisp salad, and perhaps a glass of Chablis.

$\frac{1}{2}$ cup cooked baby limas, drained
$2\frac{1}{2}$ cups fresh basil
5 oz fresh Parmesan cheese, cut in small cubes
$\frac{1}{2}$ cup olive oil
$\frac{1}{4}$ cup pine nuts, or walnuts
1 tablespoon lemon juice (optional)
1 lb spaghetti, cooked and drained

Put beans, basil, cheese, oil and nuts in food processor. Process till smooth. If too thick, add a little more oil. If desired, a tablespoon of lemon juice can be added. Serve over hot cooked spaghetti.

Makes about 2 cups pesto sauce, 4 to 6 servings.

Shepherd's Pie

Here's a thrifty meal that used to be popular among British working classes, and is still widely available for lunch in British "pubs." In this adaptation, beans, vegetables and potatoes combine in a casserole that's hearty enough for large appetites.

 1 cup cooked cranberry beans, drained
 1/2 cup celery, finely chopped
 1/2 cup zucchini, thinly sliced
 1 cup whole-kernel canned corn
 1/2 cup cauliflower, cut in small pieces
 1 cup fresh green beans, cut in 1-inch pieces
 1 cup carrots, thinly sliced
 1 (10-oz) can cream of mushroom soup
 2 cups low-fat milk
 2 teaspoons onion powder
 1/2 teaspoon *each* thyme and salt
 2 cups cooked potatoes, mashed with 1/4 cup milk and
      3 tablespoons butter or margarine (if too dry, add
      more milk)
 1/2 teaspoon paprika

In a large 4- or 5-quart casserole, mix all ingredients except potatoes and paprika. When everything is thoroughly mixed, spoon on mashed potatoes, creating a ring around the outer edge, leaving a center opening for steam to escape. Sprinkle paprika atop potatoes.

Bake at 350 degrees F for 35 to 45 minutes till potatoes are golden and bubbly.

Makes 4 to 6 servings.

Soldier Croquettes with Mushroom Sauce

The cornmeal in these croquettes brings out the flavor of Southern cooking and adds a lovely crunch.

>1 lb European Soldier beans, cooked, drained and
>   mashed
>2 eggs, well beaten
>$1/4$ cup milk
>1 small onion, minced
>1 garlic clove, minced
>2 tablespoons fresh parsley, finely chopped
>$1/2$ teaspoon *each* salt and freshly ground black pepper
>$1/2$ cup yellow cornmeal
>Oil for frying
>Sprigs of parsley for garnish
>1 recipe Mushroom Sauce (recipe follows)

In a medium bowl, mash beans, add eggs, milk, onion, garlic, parsley and seasonings. Blend well, and stir in cornmeal. Form into croquette shapes.

In a large fry pan, heat oil and brown croquettes on both sides. Drain well on paper towels. Serve hot, garnished with parsley sprigs and accompanied by a sauceboat of mushroom sauce.

For *Mushroom Sauce*, please turn page.

Mushroom Sauce (Makes 1$^1/_2$ to 2 cups)

    8 oz fresh mushrooms, sliced
    3 tablespoons butter or margarine
    3 tablespoons all-purpose flour
    1 teaspoon onion powder
    1 cup half & half
    1 teaspoon Bernard Jensen's Broth or Seasoning
        (vegetable mix found in most health-food stores)
    Salt and freshly ground black pepper to taste

In a medium pan, sauté mushrooms in butter or margarine. Cook about 5 minutes on low heat. Stir in flour and onion powder. Cook about 5 more minutes, gradually adding half & half and seasonings. Stir till sauce is of gravy texture, heating gently but thoroughly.

Makes 4 to 6 servings.

Spinach Soybean Soufflé

This soufflé makes an attractive main dish that your luncheon guests will rave about. Serve with hot crisp rolls and a chilled dry white wine.

$1/4$ cup butter or margarine
$1/4$ cup all-purpose flour
$1/2$ teaspoon salt
1 cup milk
1 teaspoon onion powder
$1/4$ teaspoon ground nutmeg
3 eggs, separated
$1/4$ teaspoon cream of tartar
1 cup cooked soybeans, drained
1 (10-oz) package frozen chopped spinach, thawed and
     thoroughly drained
1 recipe Mushroom Sauce (see recipe, Page 142)

In a medium pan, melt butter or margarine and blend in flour and salt. Cook over low heat till smooth. Stir in milk and heat till boiling, stirring constantly. Boil and stir for 1 minute. Remove from heat, add onion powder and nutmeg.

In a small bowl, beat egg whites and cream of tartar until stiff. In a smaller bowl, beat egg yolks till thick.

Stir yolks into white sauce mixture in pan and add beans and spinach. Stir in about one quarter of egg whites. Gently fold in rest of egg whites. Pour into a $1^1/2$-quart buttered soufflé or casserole dish. Set soufflé dish in a pan of water 1 inch deep.

Bake at 350 degrees F for 50 to 60 minutes, until an inserted knife blade comes out clean. Serve immediately with hot Mushroom Sauce.

Makes 4 to 6 servings.

Vegetable Bean Lasagna

A great crowd pleaser and a complete meal in one pan. This dish has always been a family favorite.

    1 medium onion, chopped
    3 garlic cloves, mashed
    2 tablespoons olive oil
    1 cup cooked Madeira beans, drained and processed to
        coarse meal in food processor
    1 (16-oz) can diced tomatoes
    1 (8-oz) can tomato sauce
    ½ cup dry red wine
    1 teaspoon *each* dried oregano, basil and rosemary
    Salt and freshly ground black pepper to taste
    16 oz ricotta cheese
    3 eggs
    1 (10-oz) package frozen chopped spinach, thawed and
        drained
    ½ lb fresh mushrooms, thinly sliced
    4 small zucchini, thinly sliced
    4 stalks broccoli, cut in small pieces
    2 medium carrots, thinly sliced
    1 lb lasagna noodles, cooked and drained, following
        directions on package
    8 oz shredded mozzarella cheese
    ½ cup freshly grated Parmesan cheese

In a large pot, sauté onion and garlic in olive oil till translucent. Add beans, diced tomatoes, tomato sauce, red wine, oregano, basil and rosemary. Cover and let simmer for about 1 hour, and add salt and black pepper to taste.

In a small bowl, blend ricotta cheese, eggs and spinach. Set aside.

In a medium bowl, toss together mushrooms, zucchini, broccoli and carrots. Set aside.

To assemble: in the bottom of a buttered 9" x 13" x 2" pan, arrange about one third of the cooked noodles. Spread about one third of the tomato-bean mixture on top, then one third of the ricotta-spinach mixture. Then sprinkle one third of the mozzarella cheese and one third of the mushroom mixture atop ricotta-spinach mixture. Repeat this layering two more times. Top with Parmesan cheese.

Bake at 350 degrees F for 30 to 45 minutes till bubbly. Let cool slightly to make it easier to cut and serve.

Makes 6 to 8 servings.

Side Dishes

To round out a meal, or accompany a salad for a light supper, beans make superb partners, adding color and flavor interest. In many cases, any leftover beans served as a side dish at one meal can be tossed into soups or salads the following day, to create great new flavor combinations.

Black Bean Pancakes
Cholent
Chutney Cowpeas
Creole Favorite
Garbanzos and Rice
Happy Valentines
International Beans
Italian Flag
Rattlesnake Ring
Stuffed Squash
Twice Baked and Stuffed Potatoes

Black Bean Pancakes

When you want a change from potatoes and you're tired of rice and pasta, these savory pancakes make a novel alternative.

1 cup cooked black turtle beans, drained and mashed
$\frac{1}{4}$ cup water
2 tablespoons dry sherry
2 eggs, well beaten
$\frac{1}{3}$ cup all-purpose flour
2 tablespoons vegetable oil
$\frac{1}{4}$ cup scallions, finely minced
1 garlic clove, peeled and finely minced
1 tablespoon fresh parsley, chopped
$\frac{1}{2}$ teaspoon salt
2 good turns of a black-pepper mill, or to taste
Vegetable oil spray to grease fry pan

Spin beans with water and sherry in a food processor until smooth. In a large bowl, place bean mixture with remaining ingredients and blend thoroughly. Lightly spray a heavy fry pan with oil and heat until hot. For each pancake, pour a tablespoon of batter onto fry pan and cook till edges begin to brown, about 45 seconds over medium-high heat. Flip over with a spatula and cook other side for about 30 seconds. Keep cooked pancakes warm and covered while remainder of batter is being used.

Makes about 6 pancakes.

Cholent

A traditional peasant dish popular throughout Middle and Eastern Europe. Although this one uses pinto and white beans, it can be made with many other varieties. Tasty, economical and filling, it's a dish that can stretch into many meals, depending on the state of your budget.

> 1 cup dried pinto beans, soaked and drained
> 1 cup white beans (Great Northerns, limas or haricots), soaked and drained
> 1 large onion
> 2 large garlic cloves, mashed
> 2 tablespoons butter or margarine
> $1/2$ cup white pearl barley
> $1^1/_2$ to 2 teaspoons liquid smoke seasoning
> 2 teaspoons seasoned salt
> 2 teaspoons freshly ground black pepper

In a large pot, place pinto and white beans with water to cover. Let come to boil. Reduce flame to low. Sauté onions and garlic in butter till translucent, and add to beans and cook for about 2 hours or until beans are tender. Add water as needed. Add barley, liquid smoke, seasoned salt and pepper. Cook on low heat for another hour until barley is tender and the liquid is absorbed.

Makes 8 servings.

Chutney Cowpeas

Cowpeas were originally grown in India as well as Asia. Inspired by Indian cuisine, this recipe uses fruit chutney to give a spiciness reminiscent of flavor combinations found on the Indian subcontinent. Since chutneys can vary and be fiery hot for American tastes, adjust the mustard and ginger to your liking.

> 1 lb cowpeas, drained and cooked
> 1 cup water
> 1/2 cup butter or margarine, melted
> 4 tablespoons corn syrup
> 2/3 cup chutney (mango, pineapple, peach, ginger or
>   any other commercial flavor found in health-food
>   stores, or some supermarkets)
> 1/4 to 1/2 teaspoon dry mustard
> 1/4 to 1/2 teaspoon ground ginger

In a large bowl, mix the cowpeas with all the other ingredients. Place in 2-quart casserole dish. Add more water if necessary to just cover bean-chutney mixture.

Bake at 325 degrees F for 1 hour to heat thoroughly and blend flavors.

Makes 4 to 6 servings.

Creole Favorite

According to Creole custom, red beans and rice and laundry were always done on Mondays. This dish takes four hours to cook—time enough to get the laundry done!

  1 lb dried scarlet runner beans, soaked overnight and
    drained
  2 medium onions, chopped
  1 bunch scallions, chopped
  1 medium red bell pepper, seeded and chopped
  2 ribs celery, chopped
  4 bay leaves
  $1/_2$ teaspoon dried thyme
  $1/_4$ teaspoon cayenne pepper
  2 turns of a black-pepper mill
  1 to $1^1/_2$ teaspoons liquid smoke seasoning
  Salt to taste
  3 cups hot cooked rice

In a large pan, place beans with water to cover and cook to a boil. Add all ingredients except salt and rice. Lower heat and simmer for 4 hours or until tender. Remove from heat and remove bay leaves. Add salt to taste. Serve over hot cooked rice.

Makes 6 servings.

Garbanzos and Rice

This is an intriguing sweet side dish that's definitely different.
Serve as a vegetable with baked eggplant and asparagus.

The recipe is versatile as you can also enjoy it as a dessert,
served warm in tall stemmed glasses, garnished with fresh orange
slices and thin crisp wafer cookies.

> 1½ cups cooked or canned garbanzo beans
> 2 cups cooked rice
> 1 teaspoon salt
> 1 teaspoon butter or margarine
> ⅓ cup honey
> ⅓ cup brown sugar
> ¼ teaspoon cinnamon

Combine all ingredients except cinnamon in a medium-
size bowl, then pour into a casserole dish. Dust with
the cinnamon.

Bake at 350 degrees F for 25 minutes.

Makes 4 to 6 servings.

Happy Valentines

These handsome Black Valentine beans have a wonderful flavor accentuated by the corn, tomatoes and cheese.

　　　2 cups cooked Black Valentine beans, drained
　　　1 (28-oz) can crushed tomatoes
　　　1 teaspoon sugar
　　　1 teaspoon garlic powder
　　　1 tablespoon onion powder
　　　$1/2$ teaspoon salt
　　　2 cups canned whole-kernel corn, drained
　　　1 cup fine bread crumbs
　　　$1/2$ cup grated Cheddar cheese

Place a layer of beans on the bottom of a large casserole dish. In a small bowl, mix tomatoes, sugar and seasonings together and spoon some over bean layer. Add layer of corn. Alternate layers. Top with bread crumbs and sprinkle with cheese.

Bake at 375 degrees F for about 30 minutes or until cheese topping is bubbly.

Makes 6 to 8 servings.

International Beans

A versatile dish with many possibilities: make it Mexican, using chili powder and cumin; or switch to Italian, substituting oregano and basil.

> 1 large onion, chopped
> 2 garlic cloves, mashed
> $1/4$ cup oil (make it olive oil for Italian style)
> 2 cups cooked Anasazi beans, drained
> 4 cups water
> 4 medium tomatoes, chopped
> $1/4$ teaspoon cayenne pepper
> *Mexican* seasoning:
>   2 teaspoons New Mexican-style chili powder
>   1 teaspoon cumin
> or:
> *Italian* seasoning:
>   1 tablespoon crushed oregano
>   2 teaspoons dried basil

Brown onion and garlic in oil till translucent. Add beans, water, tomatoes and appropriate seasonings. Cook over low heat for 45 minutes.

Makes 4 to 6 servings.

Italian Flag

Unveil the flag colors of green, white and red with this side dish that's fabulous with Italian food—perhaps to commemorate Columbus Day!

2 garlic cloves, minced
2 scallions, coarsely chopped
1 medium red bell pepper, seeded and coarsely
    chopped
2 oz ($^1/_4$ stick) butter or margarine
$^1/_2$ lb to $^3/_4$ lb white Dixie butter beans, cooked and
    drained
Salt and freshly ground black pepper to taste

In a small pan, sauté garlic, scallions and bell pepper in butter or margarine. In a medium bowl, mix garlic mixture with beans and seasonings to taste. Serve warm.

Makes 4 to 6 servings.

Rattlesnake Ring

This one is easy to toss together, it looks most attractive, and it tastes good. Made in a mold pan, the serving platter can be beautifully decorated for a small buffet luncheon.

$1/2$ cup cooked rattlesnake beans, well drained
$1/2$ cup pecans, chopped
2 ribs celery, chopped
1 tablespoon fresh parsley, chopped
1 small onion, chopped
$1/2$ green, red or yellow bell pepper, seeded and
    chopped
1 cup bread crumbs
3 eggs, well beaten
4 tablespoons butter or margarine, melted
$1^1/2$ cups low-fat milk
$1/2$ teaspoon *each* salt and freshly ground black pepper

Place everything in food processor and blend to a coarse meal. Pour mixture into an oil-sprayed or buttered 6-cup ring mold. Put ring mold in a larger pan filled with hot water to halfway up ring mold (to prevent drying out).

Bake at 350 degrees F for 1 hour. Let stand 10 minutes before unmolding.

Makes 4 to 6 servings.

Stuffed Squash

A wonderful mixture of flavors and colors, with the beans-and-rice combination giving a bonus of complete protein.

> 2 small buttercup or acorn squash
> 1/2 cup cooked peanut beans
> 1/2 cup cooked Basmati rice
> 2 tablespoons onion flakes
> 1 tablespoon parsley flakes
> 2 teaspoons garlic powder
> Salt and freshly ground black pepper to taste
> 1 cup vegetable bouillon
> 10 whole almonds

Prick squash with a fork in several places and place on paper towel in microwave oven. Cook about 12 minutes on full heat, rotating halfway through cooking. Cut squash in half. Remove and discard seedy center.

Scoop out squash pulp and place in a medium bowl. Stir in beans, rice, onion flakes, parsley flakes, garlic powder and seasonings. Mix well and stir in vegetable bouillon. Refill scooped out squash with the bean-rice mixture. Stud whole almonds on each squash. Place in a greased baking dish.

Bake at 350 degrees F for 20 to 25 minutes.

Makes 2 to 4 servings.

Twice Baked and Stuffed Potatoes

Once-baked potatoes are always good. *Twice*-baked and stuffed with beans and veggies, they taste *doubly* good! Potatoes can be prepared in advance and reheated just before serving. Any potatoes left over will freeze well—but they rarely are left over!

4 baked potatoes
1 cup cooked butter beans, drained
1 medium onion, chopped
1 carrot, diced
$\frac{1}{2}$ lb fresh green beans, cut into $\frac{1}{2}$-inch pieces
1 stalk broccoli (flower top only), cut into small pieces
3 tablespoons butter or margarine
1 (10-oz) can cream of celery soup
$\frac{1}{2}$ cup low-fat milk
Paprika

Cut potatoes in half. Scoop potato from skins, being careful to keep shells intact. In a medium bowl, mash potatoes thoroughly with beans, and set aside.

Sauté onion, carrot, green beans and broccoli in butter till onion becomes translucent. Add to potato-bean mixture. Stir celery soup with milk and add to mixture. Mix thoroughly and return to potato halves. Place in a greased baking dish and dust generously with paprika.

Bake at 350 degrees F for 20 to 25 minutes. Or microwave on high power for 3 to 4 minutes.

Makes 8 servings as a side dish, or 4 servings as a main dish.

Desserts

Don't laugh—they're fantastic! When family or friends claim emphatically that they don't like beans, these delicious treats can be a foxy way to introduce them in meals and snacks!

Bakewell Tarts
Bean Fritters
Beanie Brownies
Chocolate Beans
Coconut Bean Balls
Health-Nut Muffins
Manchurian Pie
Pear Lima Dessert Casserole with Frozen Cream
Spice Cake
Whippoorwill Gingerbread Cake

Bakewell Tarts

These lightly filled, delicate pastries are inspired by the tarts
served at four o'clock teatime in England. They can be served as a
dainty dessert after a main course, accompanied by a special
espresso or an almond-flavored herbal tea to enhance their flavor.
Experiment with various fruit jams to create different effects.

> 1 recipe pie crust (recipe below)
> $1\frac{1}{2}$ cups cooked European Soldier beans, drained
> $\frac{1}{2}$ cup mild honey
> 1 teaspoon almond extract
> Apricot jam

Prepare pie crust. Roll out pie crust dough until thin,
and cut 36 circles with a round cutter. Set aside.

Process beans, honey and almond extract in a food
processor to the consistency of thick apple sauce.

To assemble: place 12 pastry circles in a mini-tart
pan, fill each with $\frac{1}{2}$ teaspoon bean mixture and top
with $\frac{1}{2}$ teaspoon apricot jam.

Bake at 375 degrees F for 20 minutes. Remove and
dust with confectioner's sugar while still warm, if
desired.

Pie crust

> 4 oz (1 stick) margarine
> $1\frac{1}{4}$ cups unsifted flour
> 2 tablespoons *ice*-cold water
> 1 teaspoon sugar
> Sprinkle of salt

Mix all ingredients together and chill till cold.

Makes 36 mini-tarts.

Bean Fritters

This is Southern cooking at its best—a wonderful dessert to finish a light meal.

> 1 cup cooked small white navy beans, drained
> 1 cup low-fat milk
> ½ cup flour
> 1 egg, well beaten
> ½ teaspoon sugar
> 1 teaspoon baking powder
> Oil for frying

In a medium bowl, mix together everything but the oil. Coarsely purée the mixture in food processor.

Heat about 2 inches of oil in a deep fry pan. Drop batter by tablespoonfuls into hot oil. Cook till crisp and golden brown on both sides. Remove fritters with a slotted spoon and drain well on paper towels. Serve hot with warmed maple syrup or honey.

Makes about 12 fritters.

Beanie Brownies

A rich, moist brownie, so terrific you'll probably want to make a double batch. No one will guess their secret goodness is tepary beans. Carob powder is made from pods of the carob tree, processed to resemble cocoa powder. However, carob contains more nutrients and is caffeine free. It is sold in health-food stores.

1 cup cooked brown tepary beans
$1/2$ cup carob powder
$3/4$ cup mild honey
$1/4$ cup margarine, melted
$1/2$ cup all-purpose flour
$1/2$ cup chopped walnuts
$1/2$ cup raisins (optional)
2 eggs, well beaten
$1^1/_2$ teaspoons vanilla essence
$1/2$ teaspoon salt

Butter an 8-inch square pan. Line pan with waxed paper and butter the paper.

Whirl the tepary beans in a food processor until smooth. In a large bowl, mix the processed beans with rest of ingredients. Spread in prepared baking dish.

Bake at 325 degrees F for 30 to 35 minutes. Cool before removing from pan. Peel off waxed paper and cut into squares.

Makes 16 2-inch squares.

Chocolate Beans

We've all tasted chocolate-covered almonds, or strawberries elegantly dipped in chocolate, or (for the brave-hearted!) chocolate-covered grasshoppers. But here's a special treat —chocolate-coated beans.

> 1 (8-oz) bar sweet chocolate
> 2 cups cooked and cooled lupini beans (baby favas) (or
>   any large mild-flavored white bean such as limas)
> Rounded toothpicks

Melt chocolate over hot water in a double boiler and allow to cool. Pierce each bean with a toothpick and dip into chocolate. Place on waxed paper to harden. For a richer taste, give each bean a double dipping.

Makes about 2½ cups.

Coconut Bean Balls

These nutty-flavored balls will be fabulous at a high tea or with that special cup of coffee, when you want a little something that's light, sweet and not too filling.

> ³/₄ cup butter or margarine, melted
> 2 cups instant powdered milk
> 1½ cups powdered confectioner's sugar
> ½ cup cooked soybeans, cooled, drained and puréed
> ¼ cup flaked coconut
> ¼ cup raisins

In a medium bowl mix melted butter with dried milk and sugar, and stir until creamy. Mix in bean purée, coconut and raisins. If too moist, add a little more dried milk; if too dry, add a little more melted butter. Roll into balls about 1-inch diameter.

Makes 36 1-inch balls.

Health-Nut Muffins

Enriched with molasses, nuts and dried fruit, these moist and wholesome muffins are high in both soluble and insoluble fiber, and good any time of the day. They're perfect for a light breakfast, a leisurely Sunday brunch, as an accompaniment to dinner, for youngsters to snack on with a mug of hot chocolate after school, or with a glass of milk at bedtime. Better make up two batches—one for now and one to freeze for later.

  1 cup 100% Bran cereal
  1¼ cups low-fat milk
  1 cup cooked brown tepary beans, drained
  ⅓ cup brown sugar, well packed
  1 tablespoon molasses
  1 egg
  ¼ cup (½ stick) butter or margarine, melted
  1 cup unsifted all-purpose flour
  2 teaspoons baking powder
  ½ teaspoon *each* baking soda and salt
  ½ cup *each* chopped walnuts and raisins

In a large bowl, combine bran with 1 cup of the milk and leave for 5 minutes.

In a food processor, process tepary beans with the remaining ¼ cup milk, then add to bran mixture. Add brown sugar, molasses, melted margarine and egg, and beat well. Fold in gently the flour, baking powder, baking soda, salt. Add nuts and raisins. Spoon batter into 2½-inch muffin tins lined with waxed-paper cases.

Bake at 400 degrees F for 20 to 25 minutes. Serve warm with butter.

Individual muffins in paper cases reheat easily in just 30 seconds on full power in the microwave. In the conventional oven, and wrapped in aluminum foil, they reheat in about 15 minutes at 350 degrees F.

Makes about 16 2½-inch muffins.

Manchurian Pie

You'll be proud to serve this delectable pie at your Thanksgiving table. It tastes incredibly like pumpkin.

     1 9-inch pastry shell, unbaked (homemade or
        ready-made)
     2 cups well-cooked soybeans
     ¾ cup honey
     2 large eggs, slightly beaten
     ½ cup milk
     4 tablespoons instant dried milk
     1 teaspoon cinnamon
     ¼ teaspoon cloves
     ¾ teaspoon ginger
     ¾ teaspoon nutmeg
     Salt to taste
     Whipped cream for topping

Spin soybeans in a food processor or blender to make 1½ cups purée. Mix ingredients in a medium-size bowl and pour into unbaked pie shell.

   Bake at 450 degrees F for 15 minutes, then reduce heat to 350 degrees F and bake 30 minutes longer, or until a knife inserted in the center comes out clean. Cool slightly before serving with a whipped cream topping.

Makes a 9-inch pie, about 6 to 8 servings.

Pear Lima Dessert Casserole with Frozen Cream

Long slow cooking makes a great blend of two very different ingredients—sweet pears and buttery-textured Christmas lima beans—with the beans contributing attractive color.

> 1 cup whipping cream
> 1 lb Christmas lima beans, cooked and drained
> 1 (29-oz) can pear halves in syrup
> $\frac{1}{2}$ cup butter or margarine, melted
> 1 cup brown sugar

The night before, whip cream until stiff. Arrange tablespoonfuls of cream on a large cookie sheet and freeze until firm. Store in freezer in plastic bags until ready to garnish dessert.

Butter a large casserole dish and line the bottom with a layer of cooked beans. Drain canned pears, reserving $\frac{1}{3}$ cup of pear syrup, and cut pears into small cubes. In a small bowl, mix together melted butter, brown sugar and pear syrup. Spread a portion onto beans. Add a layer of pear cubes. Spread each layer with butter-sugar mixture. Alternate layers, ending with pears on top. Spread with remaining butter-sugar mixture. Cover.

Bake at 325 degrees F for 1 hour. Serve warm, garnished with frozen whipped cream.

Makes 6 servings.

Spice Cake

A flavorful cake, proving that beans can enhance the taste and improve the texture of almost any food.

$\frac{1}{4}$ cup ($\frac{1}{2}$ stick) butter or margarine, softened
1 cup mild honey
1 egg, well beaten
2 teaspoons vanilla essence
2 cups cooked pinquito beans, puréed
1 cup all-purpose flour
1 teaspoon baking soda
$\frac{1}{2}$ teaspoon salt
1 teaspoon each allspice and cinnamon
2 cups finely-diced apples, peeled
1 cup golden raisins
Confectioner's sugar

In a large bowl, beat butter and honey until creamy, then add egg and vanilla. Stir in bean purée. Sift flour, soda, salt and spices, and add to mixture. Add apples and golden raisins and mix well. Pour into 9" x 13" greased pan.

Bake at 375 degrees F for about 45 minutes, until a test toothpick comes out clean. Let cool. Dust with confectioner's sugar and cut into squares.

Makes about 20 2½" x 4" servings.

Whippoorwill Gingerbread Cake

The lovely fragrance of this spicy gingerbread will fill the kitchen while it bakes. Gingerbread can be enjoyed fresh and warm from the oven with a steaming cup of coffee; or it can be sliced for dessert, topped with fresh or canned peach slices and English Toffee ice cream.

$1/2$ cup dried whippoorwill beans
1 cup molasses
$1/3$ cup butter or margarine
$1/2$ cup sour milk
1 egg
$1^1/_2$ cups all-purpose flour
$1^1/_2$ teaspoons *each* baking soda and ground ginger
$1/2$ teaspoon salt

Soak whippoorwills overnight. Drain and replace water occasionally if you can. With fresh hot water, cook them 2 hours or until very tender and mushy. Drain, reserving the cooking liquid. Process beans in a food processor with $1/4$ cup reserved liquid.

In a small pan, heat together molasses and butter or margarine. Cool.

In a medium bowl, mix molasses mixture with sour milk and egg. Sift together flour, soda, ginger and salt, and stir gently into molasses mixture, then add bean purée. Beat just enough to make a smooth batter. Spoon into an 8- or 9-inch square buttered baking pan.

Bake at 325 degrees F for about 35 minutes. Cool slightly in pan before removing and cutting into 2-inch squares.

Makes 16 2-inch squares.

Legumes of the World

This appendix will help you identify the principal legumes sold in the United States. Some type of bean is important in almost every country or area of the world. These countries are listed under the specific bean names together with the main U.S. growing areas, where known. Names for beans can vary from region to region and from store to store, sometimes depending on local preferences.

Sizes of beans, peas and lentils are only approximate, since they can vary according to area, soil type, climate, and methods of cultivation.

The availability of legumes can depend on where you live and the quantities produced each season. If you cannot find certain beans in local markets, many specialty food stores listed in Appendix 2 will sell legumes by mail order. The widest selections are usually in stock in September and October after the summer harvest has been sorted, cleaned, graded and made ready for marketing.

Cooking times for dried beans, peas and lentils are approximate; they vary greatly depending on size, variety, freshness and storage conditions, and also whether you want beans to retain their shape for a salad or to cook longer for a dip or purée. A pressure cooker can radically cut down cooking time. See Chapter 5 for full details on preparation.

Adzuki bean *(Phaseolus angularis)*, also called Adsuki, aduki, asuki, azuki, feijao, Tiensin red, field pea, red oriental bean. Important in China, Japan, Korea and Manchuria.

Small, about $1/4$-inch long; light brown or dark reddish brown color with black/white ridge. Somewhat sweet nut-like flavor. Use as a vegetable side dish, tossed with butter, or in salads combined with tomatoes, coriander, cumin and garlic. Or try a salad of adzukis tossed with watercress, tamari, wasabi and sesame oil. Makes a sweet bean paste used in desserts and cakes.

Sold in Chinese, Japanese, Indian, health-food stores and specialty food stores.

Soak at least 4 hours or overnight; or quick-soak. Cook 1 hour. Or pressure cook (soaked) 15 mins., (unsoaked) 20 mins.

Anasazi® bean. Related to the kidney bean (Phaseolus vulgaris). Cultivation of this bean can be traced back to the Anasazi Indians of Southwest U.S. one thousand years ago. Now grown in Colorado.

About $1/2$-inch long, kidney-shaped. Dappled purple and cream, the color fades to a uniform dark pink after cooking.

Sold in health-food stores and specialty food stores.

No soaking is necessary, but it will accelerate cooking time.

Soak at least 4 hours or overnight; or quick-soak. Cook about 1 hour. Or pressure cook (soaked) 20 mins., (unsoaked) 25 mins.

Appaloosa bean. Related to the kidney bean *(Phaseolus vulgaris).*

Grown in California, Idaho and Vermont.

About $1/2$-inch long, with black/brown spots on light background, similar to marks on Appaloosa ponies. This bean is good in chili, or may be cooked and mashed with hot sauce or mustard, as a side dish.

Sold by specialty food stores.

Soak at least 4 hours or overnight; or quick-soak. Cook 1 to $1^1/_2$ hours. Or pressure cook (soaked) 20 mins., (unsoaked) 25 mins.

Baby lima bean *(Phaseolus lunatus).* Dwarf variety of the lima bean. Also called sieva bean. *See* also Lima bean.

Origin: tropical America. Grown in California.

About $1/2$-inch long. Dried baby limas are usually white; frozen baby limas are usually pale green. Delicate sweet flavor.

Sold in supermarkets. Other unusual colorations are sold in Hispanic markets and specialty food stores.

Soak at least 4 hours or overnight; or quick-soak. Cook 1 hour. Or pressure cook (soaked) 20 mins., (unsoaked) 25 to 30 mins.

Baccicia bean. Related to the kidney bean *(Phaseolus vulgaris).*

About $1/2$-inch long, dark red, sometimes dappled with cream. Color pales after soaking and cooking. Old-fashioned Italian garden bean, popular in Europe.

Sold by specialty food stores.

Soak at least 4 hours or overnight; or quick-soak. Cook 1 to $1^1/_2$ hours. Or pressure cook (soaked) 20 mins., (unsoaked) 25 mins.

Bell bean. Related to broad bean *(Vicia faba).* Also called baby fava bean, *ful nabed.* See the note on Favism in Chapter 4.

Common in Egypt. Grown in California.

About $1/2$-inch long with flat shape; cream or light brown.

Sold by specialty food stores.

Soak 12 hours. Cook 3 hours. Or pressure cook (soaked) 40 mins., (unsoaked) 1 hour.

Black bean. Related to the kidney bean *(Phaseolus vulgaris)*. Also called turtle bean, negro bean, Mexican black, and Spanish black.

Grown in Michigan, New York and Southern U.S. Also Caribbean, Mexico and South America.

About $3/8$-inch long, oval-shaped, with black skin and creamy interior. Full earthy-mushroom flavor and somewhat mealy texture. Basic for many Caribbean and Latin American soups and side dishes. This bean is marvelous in thick soups or with rice; usually seasoned with coriander, cumin and garlic, and topped with sour cream, chopped red onion and fresh cilantro.

Available canned cooked or dried. Sold in many supermarkets, Hispanic markets and health-food stores.

Soak at least 4 hours or overnight; or quick-soak. Cook $1^1/_2$ hours. Or pressure cook (soaked) 15 mins., (unsoaked) 20 mins.

Black-eyed pea. *(Vigna unguiculata,* formerly *V. sinensis).* A cowpea, related to the mung bean. Also called black-eyed bean, cowpea, field pea, Tonkin pea, China pea, marble pea, brown-eyed pea, Jerusalem pea, black-eyed Suzy, *lobhia.*

Native of China. Grown in California, Idaho and Southern U.S. Also Africa, India, China, and West Indies.

About $3/8$-inch long, having a cream skin with a distinctive black or yellow dot. Sweet mild pea-like flavor; absorbs other flavors. Popular in Southern cuisine. Used (with rice) in dishes such as Hoppin' John served

New Year's Day with a shiny dime added for luck. In India, these peas are ground into flour for crepes and pancakes.

Available canned cooked, frozen or dried. Sold in many supermarkets.

No soaking is necessary. Cook 30 mins. to 1 hour. Or pressure cook 10 mins.

Black gram. *(Phaseolus mungo* or *Vigna mungo).* Also called urd beans, *sabat, kali dal* and *urad dal. Urad dal* usually refers to the hulled ivory-white seed.

Grown since ancient times in India and also Southeast Asia. Used for making wafers called *papad* or *puppadam.* Easy to digest.

Sold in Indian markets, Middle Eastern stores or specialty food stores.

No soaking is necessary. Cook 30 mins. Or pressure cook 8 mins.

Black runner bean. Related to the scarlet runner bean *(Phaseolus coccineus).*

Grown in California.

About $7/_8$-inch long; a handsome glossy black. Good flavor with a tender skin.

Sold by specialty food stores.

Soak at least 4 hours or overnight; or quick-soak. Cook $1\frac{1}{2}$ hours. Or pressure cook (soaked) 20 mins., (unsoaked) 25 mins.

Black Valentine bean. Related to the kidney bean *(Phaseolus vulgaris).*

Grown in California.

About $5/_8$-inch long, kidney-shaped; glossy black. Rich meaty flavor and mealy texture. Makes a hearty soup.

Sold by specialty food stores.

Soak at least 4 hours or overnight; or quick-soak.

Cook 1 to $1\frac{1}{2}$ hours. Or pressure cook (soaked) 20 mins., (unsoaked) 25 mins.

Bolito. Related to the kidney bean *(Phaseolus vulgaris)*. Also called bollito, bolita.

Grown and used in New Mexico.

Size of a large pea; milk chocolate or light brown color. Easier to cook than pinto beans.

Sold in Hispanic markets or specialty food stores.

Soak at least 4 hours or overnight; or quick-soak. Cook about 1 hour. Or pressure cook (soaked) 20 mins., (unsoaked) 25 mins.

Broad bean. *(Vicia faba). See* Fava bean.

Brown bean. *(Vigna acontifolius).* Also called *Moth dal.*

Widely grown in India.

Tiny brownish green seed, the size of chocolate sprinkles. Used as popular snacks in India.

Sold in Indian markets.

Soak at least 4 hours or overnight; or quick-soak. Drain and then fry.

Butter bean. *See* Lima bean.

Calypso bean. Related to the kidney bean *(Phaseolus vulgaris)*.

About $\frac{3}{8}$-inch long; dramatic black and white markings. An exciting addition to cassoulets, soups and stews; a silky smooth texture for purées.

Sold by specialty food stores.

Soak at least 4 hours or overnight; or quick-soak. Cook 1 to $1\frac{1}{2}$ hours. Or pressure cook (soaked) 20 mins., (unsoaked) 25 mins.

Cannellini bean. Related to the kidney bean *(Phaseolus vulgaris)*. Also called fasolia.

Originally cultivated in Argentina; widely grown in Italy.

A $1/2$-inch long ivory-white bean. Smooth texture and subtle nut-like flavor. Classic for savory Italian dishes such as minestrone or Tuscan tuna and white bean salad.

Available canned cooked or dried. Sold in many supermarkets, or specialty food stores. *See* White bean.

Soak at least 4 hours or overnight; or quick-soak. Cook 1 to $1^{1}/_{2}$ hours. Or pressure cook (soaked) 15 mins., (unsoaked) 20 mins.

Chickpea. *(Cicer arietinum),* also called garbanzo, ceci, cici, cheechee, *pois chiche, gram, kabuli channa, safaid channa* or *channa dal. Channa dal* refers to pea when hulled and split.

Origin: India, Africa. Grown in California. Over 80 percent of the world crop is produced in India and Pakistan; remainder is grown in Mexico, Turkey and Ethiopia.

A $3/8$-inch round bean, with a tan color. Nut-like flavor and firm texture. Delicious for appetizers, soups, mixed-bean salads, marinated salads, casseroles and patés. Serve hot in an onion sauce seasoned with a dash of nutmeg. Serve cold in a vinaigrette. Or simply toss with olive oil and garlic. This bean produces the Middle Eastern *hummus* paste, with tahini, lemon juice and garlic. Ground chickpea flour *(besan)* can make fritters, dumplings and spicy breads.

Available canned cooked or dried. Sold in most supermarkets.

Soak at least 4 hours or overnight; or quick-soak. Cook 1 to $1^{1}/_{2}$ hours; for purée, cook 2 to $2^{1}/_{2}$ hours. Or pressure cook (soaked) 20 mins., (unsoaked) 25 to 30 mins.

China yellows. Related to the kidney bean *(Phaseolus vulgaris).*

About $3/8$-inch long. The slightly globular shape and

pale yellow color make this a distinctive bean. Mellow flavor and a silky texture for purées. Accentuate color and flavor by cooking with saffron threads or turmeric. Puréed with garlic, they make a delicious side dish for grilled fish.

Sold by specialty food stores.

Soak at least 4 hours or overnight; or quick-soak. Cook 1 to $1\frac{1}{2}$ hours. Or pressure cook (soaked) 20 mins., (unsoaked) 25 to 30 mins.

Christmas lima bean. Related to the lima bean *(Phaseolus limensis)*. Also called speckled lima, speckled butter bean and calico bean.

Grown in California.

A large $\frac{7}{8}$-inch brown/white or purple/white mottled bean with distinctive chestnut-like flavor. These already large beans swell to almost double size, and retain color markings after soaking and cooking. Can be used in stuffing. Or toss beans, cooked and drained, with sautéed onion and wild mushrooms, seasoned with tarragon.

Sold by specialty food stores.

Soak at least 4 hours or overnight; or quick-soak. Cook about $1\frac{1}{2}$ hours. Or pressure cook (soaked) 20 mins., (unsoaked) 25 to 30 mins.

Cowpea. *(Vigna unguiculata,* formerly *V. sinensis).*
See Black-eyed pea.

Cranberry bean. Related to the kidney bean *(Phaseolus vulgaris)*. Also called borlotto, crab-eye, Roman, Romano, rosecoco or saluggia.

Grown in Idaho, Michigan, Minnesota, North Dakota. Also Central and South America, Africa, Iran and Italy.

About $\frac{1}{2}$-inch long; mottled pink and beige color, although colors pale after soaking and cooking. A favorite for succotash. For a special and speedy salad, toss cooked beans with crumbled gorgonzola cheese, olive oil and a small sprinkling of chopped fresh rosemary.

Sold by specialty food stores.

Soak at least 4 hours or overnight; or quick-soak. Cook 1 to $1^1/_2$ hours. Or pressure cook (soaked) 20 mins., (unsoaked) 25 mins.

Cream pea. Related to the Cowpea *(Vigna unguiculata)*.

Grown in Texas and other Southern states.

About $^1/_4$-inch pea; dark ivory color. Used in Southern cooking. Produces a somewhat creamy consistency.

Sold by specialty food stores.

No soaking necessary. Cook 30 to 35 mins. Or pressure cook 10 mins.

Crowder pea. Related to the black-eye pea *(Vigna unguiculata)*. So called because they are densely "crowded" in the pod. Also known as Mississippi silver.

Grown in California, Louisiana and Texas.

About $^1/_4$-inch long; medium brown or black color. Used in Southern cooking.

Available frozen or dried. Sold by specialty food stores.

No soaking necessary. Cook 45 mins. Or pressure cook 10 mins.

Dal. The general name in the subcontinent of India for all beans, peas and lentils.

Sold in Indian markets.

Dixie butter peas. Related to the Cowpea *(Vigna unguiculata)*.

Grown in Texas and other Southern states.

About $^3/_8$-inch long, pea-shaped. Creamy white color; another strain is dark red with speckles. Markings retained after cooking. Delicious as a vegetable side dish.

Sold by specialty food stores.

No soaking necessary. Cook 45 mins. Or pressure cook 10 mins.

European Soldier bean. *See* Soldier bean.

Fava bean. *(Vicia faba).* Also called broad bean, English bean, Windsor bean, horse bean, field bean, Scotch bean, round bean, and *sora mame.*

See note on Favism in Chapter 4.

May have been native to Africa and southwest Asia. Grown in California. Over 70 percent of the world crop is grown in China; also produced in Egypt, Italy, United Kingdom, Morocco, Spain, Denmark, Brazil and Central America.

Large $3/_4$-inch long, with flat shape. Baby variety is $1/_2$-inch long. Cream or light brown color when dried. Strong, almost bitter flavor.

Needs long soaking.

Commonly used in Arabic, Italian and Portuguese dishes. Delicious as a vegetable, or served in stews with flank steak, tomatoes, garlic and oregano. Useful for making purées.

Available canned cooked or dried.

Sold by specialty food stores.

Soak 12 hours. Cook 3 hours. Or pressure cook (soaked) 40 mins., (unsoaked) 1 hour.

Flageolet. Immature kidney bean *(Phaseolus vulgaris).*

Grown in California and Idaho. Widely cultivated in Europe.

About $3/_8$-inch long, kidney-shaped; pale green, pale ocher or white. Color retained after soaking and cooking. Delicate flavor and texture, with tender skin. Classic for French cassoulets of lamb and vegetables. To

accompany roast lamb, toss with garlic, chervil or tarragon.

Sold by specialty food stores.

Soak 4 hours or overnight; or quick-soak. Cook 1
hour. Or pressure cook (soaked) 20 mins., (unsoaked)
25 mins.

Florida butter bean. Related to the Christmas lima *(Phaseolus limensis).*

Grown in California.

About $1/2$-inch long, flattish shape; ivory color speckled with dark brown; mild flavor.

Sold by specialty food stores.

Soak at least 4 hours or overnight; or quick-soak.
Cook 1 to $1^1/2$ hours. Or pressure cook (soaked) 20
mins., (unsoaked) 25 to 30 mins.

French horticulture bean. Related to the cranberry bean
(Phaseolus vulgaris).

Grown in California.

About $1/2$-inch long; beige color mottled with pink.

Sold by specialty food stores.

Soak at least 4 hours or overnight; or quick-soak.
Cook 1 hour. Or pressure cook (soaked) 20 mins., (unsoaked) 25 mins.

French navy bean. Related to the regular navy bean *(Phaseolus vulgaris).*

Grown in Idaho.

About $3/8$-inch long; slightly globular shape dis-
tinguishes this bean from the regular navy; white with
a tinge of green color. Outstanding bacon-like flavor.
Tender for soups; excellent for salads. Toss with olive
oil and salt to taste for a simple flavorful side dish.

Sold by specialty food stores.

Soak at least 4 hours or overnight; or quick-soak.
Cook $1^1/2$ hours. Or pressure cook (soaked) 25 mins.,
(unsoaked) 30 mins.

Garbanzo. *(Cicer arietinum). See* Chickpea.

Great Northern bean. Related to the kidney bean *(Phaseolus vulgaris). See* White bean.

Grown in Colorado, Idaho, Kansas, Nebraska and Wyoming.

About $3/8$-inch long, larger than the navy bean; white color, oval shape. Mild flavor with a mealy texture. Good in casseroles and baked beans.

Sold in most supermarkets.

Soak at least 4 hours or overnight; or quick-soak. Cook 1 hour. Or pressure cook (soaked) 20 mins., (unsoaked) 25 mins.

Haricot bean. *(Phaseolus vulgaris). See* White bean.

Jackson Wonder bean. Related to the kidney bean *(Phaseolus vulgaris).* Developed in the 1880s in Atlanta, Georgia, by Thomas Jackson.

Grown in California and Idaho.

About $5/8$-inch long, oval, flattish shape; light to dark beige mottled with violet or brown. Markings remain after soaking, but may be lost after cooking. Delicious for soups.

Sold by specialty food stores.

Soak at least 4 hours or overnight; or quick-soak. Cook 45 mins. to 1 hour. Or pressure cook (soaked) 20 mins., (unsoaked) 25 mins.

Jacob's Cattle bean. Related to the kidney bean *(Phaseolus vulgaris).* Also called trout bean.

About $5/8$-inch long with a plump kidney shape. Mottled purple and white color markings, like Guernsey cows. After cooking, the patterns fade but are still distinct. Earthy flavor with a mealy texture. For an aromatic side dish or salad, try tossing cooked, drained beans with fresh rosemary, balsamic vinegar and olive oil.

Sold by specialty food stores.

Soak at least 4 hours or overnight; or quick-soak. Cook 1 to $1\frac{1}{2}$ hours. Or pressure cook (soaked) 20 mins., (unsoaked) 25 mins.

Jumbo pinto runner bean. Related to both the pinto and the runner bean *(Phaseolus vulgaris* and *P. coccineus).*

Developed and grown in California.

About $\frac{7}{8}$-inch long; large plump bean. Brown speckles on a beige background. Particularly fine flavor.

Sold by specialty food stores.

Soak at least 4 hours or overnight; or quick-soak. Cook 1 to $1\frac{1}{2}$ hours. Or pressure cook (soaked) 20 mins., (unsoaked) 25 mins.

Kidney bean. *(Phaseolus vulgaris).* Also called French bean, Mexican bean, *habichuela, badi* (large) *rajma* and *choti* (small) *rajma.* Known as snap, string or wax bean when the pod is fresh green and not dried.

Origin: Central America and South America. Grown in California, Colorado, Idaho, Michigan, Minnesota, Montana, Nebraska, New Mexico, New York, North Dakota, and Washington. Widely grown in Brazil and China.

About $\frac{1}{2}$-inch long, kidney-shaped; brown-red color. Many other colors such as light red, red, brown, white and black varieties. Rich meaty flavor and mealy texture. Popular in chili dishes. Prominent in Latin American and Creole cuisines. The dark red kidney adds a rich color accent for salads.

Available canned cooked or dried. Sold in supermarkets.

Soak at least 4 hours or overnight; or quick-soak. Cook 1 to $1\frac{1}{2}$ hours. Or pressure cook (soaked) 20 mins., (unsoaked) 25 mins.

Lentil. *(Cajanus cajan).* Also called *toovar dal, toor dal, tur dal* and *arhar dal.*

Grown and used all over India.

About $1/4$-inch round seed, ocher-yellow in color. Makes a thick creamy purée.

Sold in Indian markets.

No soaking necessary. Cook 30 mins. Or pressure cook 8 mins.

Lentil, common. *(Lens esculenta* or *L. culinaris).*

Grown in Idaho, Montana, Oregon and Washington. Widely cultivated in India, Bangladesh, Syria, Turkey, Iran, Ethiopia, Spain and North Africa.

About $1/4$-inch flat seed; color can be yellow, grey, green or dark brown, and may be mottled. Quick cooking. Makes excellent soups and purées.

Sold in most supermarkets.

No soaking necessary. Cook 35 mins. Or pressure cook 12 mins.

Lentil, French green *(Lens culinaris).*

Grown in California and in Europe.

Less than $1/4$-inch round unhulled seed; dark green color. Delicious in lentil salads, soups, East African and Indian purées.

Sold by specialty food stores.

Soak 30 minutes. Cook 40 mins. Or pressure cook 12 mins.

Lentil, red *(Lens culinaris).* Also called *masar dal, masoor dal,* and *mussoor.*

Grown in Idaho. Widely grown in India and Egypt.

Less than $1/4$-inch flat seed; pink, red or salmon color.

Fast cooking, turning yellow when cooked. Highly aromatic, with delicate flavor. Makes colorful nutritious purées and dips, in the cuisine of Northern India, Pakistan and Afghanistan.

Sold in Indian markets or specialty food stores.

No soak. Cook 30 mins. or less. Or pressure cook 8 mins.

Lima bean *(Phaseolus limensis* or *Dolichos lablab-typicus).* Also called butter bean, curry bean, Madagascar bean, pole bean, Cape pea, val bean and *lablab. See* also Baby lima bean.

Origin: Central America. Grown in California and temperate, subtropical and tropical countries.

About 1-inch long. Dried limas are usually white; frozen fresh limas pale green. Sweet flavor, due to its high sugar content. Use as a vegetable, tossed with a little butter, or add to casseroles and soups. Good with smoked meats and cheese. This bean is essential to American succotash and Eastern European cholent.

Available canned cooked, frozen or dried. Sold in most supermarkets.

Soak at least 4 hours or overnight; or quick-soak. Cook 1 to $1\frac{1}{2}$ hours. Or pressure cook (soaked) 20 mins., (unsoaked) 25 to 30 mins.

Long bean. *(Vigna unguiculata, V. sesquipedalis,* or *Dolichos sesquipedalis).* Related to the black-eyed pea. Also called asparagus bean, yard-long bean, horn bean, chopsticks bean, yak's tail and *Dau gok.*

Origin: probably Southeast Asia. Grows wild in tropical Africa. Cultivated in Asia, Africa, China, Indonesia and some Pacific islands.

Novelty-sized pods a foot or more long. Generally eaten fresh and not dried. Slice and cook similar to green string beans. Delicious when added to stews.

Sold in Asian markets.

Lupine bean. *(Lupinus* genus*).* Distantly related to the broad bean (fava). Also called lupini, luphini. See note on Favism in Chapter 4.

Native to Southern Europe and North Africa. Grown in California. Also cultivated in Italy and many European countries.

About $1/2$-inch round, flat shape; cream color.

Sold by specialty food stores.

Soak 12 hours. Cook 3 hours. Or pressure cook (soaked) 40 mins., (unsoaked) 1 hour.

Madeira bean. Related to the cranberry bean *(Phaseolus vulgaris)* and largest in the cranberry family.

Grown in California.

About $3/4$-inch long, plump kidney shape. Beige mottled with pink. Paler color after soaking and cooking.

Sold by specialty food stores.

Soak at least 4 hours or overnight; or quick-soak. Cook 45 mins. to 1 hour. Or pressure cook (soaked) 20 mins., (unsoaked) 25 mins.

Mung bean. *(Phaseolus aureus, P. radiatus, Vigna aureus or V. radiata).* Also called mung pea, green gram bean and *sabat moong.* When husked and split, the green mung bean becomes known in India as the yellow mung, *moong dal.*

Native of India. Grown in California. India and Pakistan produce most of the world crop; it is widely grown and eaten in China, Japan, Korea and Southeast Asia.

About $1/4$-inch round; dark-olive skin with light yellow interior. Somewhat sweet flavor and soft texture. Easy to digest. Best known in the Americas and Europe for producing sprouts. Mung-bean flour is used to make bean threads or cellophane noodles.

Sold in Asian markets and health-food stores, or specialty food stores.

Soak at least 4 hours or overnight; or quick-soak. Cook 45 mins. to 1 hour. Or pressure cook (soaked) 15 mins., (unsoaked) 20 mins.

Navy bean. Related to the kidney bean *(Phaseolus vulgaris)*. Also called pea bean. *See* also White bean.

Grown in Colorado, Michigan, Minnesota, Nebraska and New Mexico.

About $3/8$-inch long; white. Mild flavor with a mealy texture.

Sold in most supermarkets.

Soak at least 4 hours or overnight; or quick-soak. Cook 2 hours. Or pressure cook (soaked) 25 mins., (unsoaked) 30 mins.

New Mexico Appaloosa bean. Related to the regular Appaloosa bean and the kidney *(Phaseolus vulgaris)*. Also called Dalmatian bean and coach dog bean.

Grown in California, Idaho and New Mexico.

About $1/2$-inch long; a spectacular pattern of black speckles on a white background. Color fades after cooking, but markings remain distinct. Earthy flavor with a mealy texture.

Sold by specialty food stores.

Soak at least 4 hours or overnight; or quick-soak. Cook 1 to $1^1/4$ hours. Or pressure cook (soaked) 20 mins., (unsoaked) 25 mins.

Nuña bean. Also called popping bean.

Grown in the high Andes Mountains of Bolivia, Ecuador and Peru.

Small bean of various colors, with peanut/popcorn flavor. Cooked and eaten like popcorn.

Sold in Hispanic markets.

Pea (Garden pea). *(Pisum sativum).* Also called *matar dal.*

A long recorded history. Now grown in Idaho, Montana, Oregon and Washington. Nearly 90 percent of the world crop is produced in China and areas of the former Soviet Union.

About $1/4$-inch round when whole; also available

split. Color may be green or yellow. Use as a vegetable side dish, tossed with olive oil or bacon, or in soups and purées.

Available fresh, canned cooked, frozen or dried. Sold in most supermarkets.

Whole dried peas: Soak at least 4 hours or overnight; or quick-soak. Cook 40 mins. Or pressure cook (soaked) 15 mins., (unsoaked) 20 mins.

Split dried peas: No soaking necessary. Cook 30 mins. Or pressure cook 10 mins.

Peanut bean. Related to the kidney bean *(Phaseolus vulgaris).*

Grown in California.

About $3/8$-inch long; red-brown color, which is retained after soaking and cooking.

Sold by specialty food stores.

Soak at least 4 hours or overnight; or quick-soak. Cook about 1 hour or less. Or pressure cook (soaked) 20 mins., (unsoaked) 25 mins.

Pigeon pea. *(Cajanus indicus).* Also called caja pea, Congo pea, gandule and goongoo pea.

Grown in southern states of the U.S. Also cultivated in India, Equatorial Africa, East and West Indies.

About $1/4$-inch round; beige color speckled with light brown, with some fading during cooking. Use as a vegetable side dish.

Available canned or dried. Sold in Hispanic, Indian and Asian markets and health-food stores, or specialty food stores.

No soaking necessary. Cook 30 to 45 mins. Or pressure cook 10 mins.

Pink bean. Related to the kidney bean *(Phaseolus vulgaris).*

Grown in California, Idaho, Montana, New Mexico

and Washington. Also cultivated in Africa, Argentina, the Caribbean and Mexico.

About $1/2$-inch, kidney-shaped; pale red or light brown color. It turns a reddish brown when cooked. A favorite of the Old West. Excellent with chili or barbecue seasonings, keeping its shape in a hot chuckwagon bean pot, or in Mexican cuisine.

Available canned, cooked or dried. Sold in supermarkets or Hispanic markets.

Soak at least 4 hours or overnight; or quick-soak. Cook 1 hour. Or pressure cook (soaked) 20 mins., (unsoaked) 25 mins.

Pink-eye/Purple hull pea. Related to the Cowpea *(Vigna unguiculata)*.

Grown in Texas and other southern states.

About $1/4$-inch; cream or ivory color with a dark dot (purple hull refers to its appearance before husking). Color retained after cooking. Use as a vegetable side dish.

Sold by specialty food stores.

No soaking necessary. Cook 45 mins. Or pressure cook 12 mins.

Pinquito bean. Related to the kidney bean *(Phaseolus vulgaris)*. Also called pinkito, poquito and Santa Maria bean.

Grown in Santa Maria area of California.

About $3/8$-inch; pinkish brown color, tender skin. Color retained after soaking and cooking. Can be used like pinto beans in Mexican cuisine.

Sold in certain area supermarkets, or specialty food stores.

Soak at least 4 hours or overnight; or quick-soak. Cook 1 to $1\frac{1}{2}$ hours. Or pressure cook (soaked) 20 mins., (unsoaked) 25 mins.

Pinto bean. Related to the kidney bean *(Phaseolus vulgaris)*.

Origin: central Mexico. Grown in California, Colorado, Idaho, Kansas, Michigan, Minnesota, Montana, Nebraska, New Mexico, North Dakota, Washington and Wyoming. Also cultivated in Chile, Kenya and Mexico.

About $1/_2$-inch bean; mottled pink and brown with yellow at the keel. Full-bodied earthy flavor and a mealy texture. Relished by fans of Mexican and Tex-Mex cuisine. Great in chili or refried beans.

Available canned or dried. Sold in supermarkets or Hispanic markets.

Soak at least 4 hours or overnight; or quick-soak. Cook 1 to $1^1/_2$ hours. Or pressure cook (soaked) 20 mins., (unsoaked) 25 mins.

Rattlesnake bean. Related to the kidney bean *(Phaseolus vulgaris)*.

Grown in Idaho.

About $3/_8$-inch, with a flat shape; mottled beige and brown color. Named for the pod shape and marking, not the bean seeds. Speckles pale during soaking and cooking. Smooth texture and fresh flavor. Ideal for purées, blended with Dijon mustard; delicious with chilis, tomatoes and seasoning.

Sold by specialty food stores.

Soak at least 4 hours or overnight; or quick-soak. Cook 45 mins. to 1 hour. Or pressure cook (soaked) 20 mins., (unsoaked) 25 mins.

Red bean. Related to the kidney bean *(Phaseolus vulgaris)*.

Grown in Idaho.

About $1/_2$-inch bright red pea-bean. This richly colored legume can add color and sparkle to salads. Try tossing the cooked, drained beans with goat cheese, olive oil and fresh rosemary.

Sold by specialty food stores.

Soak at least 4 hours or overnight; or quick-soak. Cook 1 to 1¹/₂ hours. Or pressure cook (soaked) 20 mins., (unsoaked) 25 mins.

Red Mexican bean. Related to the kidney bean (*Phaseolus vulgaris*). Also called small red and Mexican chili bean.

Grown in California and Idaho.

About ³/₈-inch long, kidney-shaped; reddish-purple color. Rich flavor for soups, salads, chili and Creole dishes, this is an outstanding bean for holding its shape and not becoming soggy. Easily absorbs salad seasonings.

Available canned cooked or dried. Sold in supermarkets.

Soak at least 4 hours or overnight; or quick-soak. Cook 1 to 1¹/₂ hours. Or pressure cook (soaked) 20 mins., (unsoaked) 25 mins.

Rosecoco bean. (*Phaseolus vulgaris*). *See* Cranberry bean.

Runner bean. (*Phaseolus coccineus*).

Origin: Central America or Mexico. Grown in California and Idaho. Also cultivated in Africa, Asia, Central America and Europe. The name comes from the growth style of the vine, running low to the ground.

About ⁵/₈-inch; deep lavender or bright red skin mottled with black. Others in this group may have colors reversed, be a handsome glossy black, or pure white. Color markings retained after cooking. Good flavor and tender skin; taste and texture similar to potatoes. White runners can have a sweetish flavor. Make a special salad with cooked, drained beans tossed with crushed garlic, quartered new potatoes and olive oil.

Sold by specialty food stores.

Soak at least 4 hours or overnight; or quick-soak. Cook 1¹/₂ hours. Or pressure cook (soaked) 20 mins., (unsoaked) 25 mins.

Scarlet runner bean. *(Phaseolus coccineus).* Named for the vivid flowers on the vine. *See* Runner bean.

Snowcap bean. Related to the kidney bean *(Phaseolus vulgaris).*

About ⅝-inch long, with large kidney shape. Half white/half Cranberry bean color (pink dapples on cream). Faintly tart tomato-like flavor. Ideal in salads; good in minestrone and other fresh vegetable soups.

Sold by specialty food stores.

Soak at least 4 hours or overnight; or quick-soak. Cook 1 to 1½ hours. Or pressure cook (soaked) 20 mins., (unsoaked) 25 mins.

Soldier bean. Related to the kidney bean *(Phaseolus vulgaris).* Also called European Soldier or Johnson bean. Grown in California and Idaho.

About ⅝-inch long, oval shape. White color with reddish-brown markings on the keel similar to a toy soldier. Patterns remain after cooking. Sweet flavor, similar to the white kidney. One of the early beans, used for baked-bean dishes in Maine and New Hampshire. For a spectacular salad, toss cooked and drained beans with goat cheese, olive oil and fresh sage. Or try them with tuna, escarole and sage.

Sold by specialty food stores.

Soak at least 4 hours or overnight; or quick soak. Cook 1 to 1½ hours. Or pressure cook (soaked) 20 mins., (unsoaked) 25 mins.

Soybean. *(Glycine max.* or *G. soja).* Also called soya, soja and *daizu.* The black variety: *kuro mame.*

Origin may be Central China. Has been used in China for five thousand years. Over 90 percent of the world crop is produced by the U.S., Brazil and China.

About ⅜-inch round pea-shaped seed of dark ivory; also black, green or brown varieties. Good in soups. Soybean flour can enrich baked products.

Sold in Asian markets, health-food stores, or specialty food stores.

Soak 12 hours. Cook 3 to 3½ hours. Or pressure cook (soaked) 30 mins., (unsoaked) 35 mins.

Spanish Tolosana bean. Related to the kidney bean *(Phaseolus vulgaris)*. Also called Prince bean.

About ½-inch long; rich purple and tan color. Handsome in salads.

Sold by specialty food stores.

Soak at least 4 hours or overnight; or quick-soak. Cook 1 to 1½ hours. Or pressure cook (soaked) 20 mins., (unsoaked) 25 mins.

Speckled butter bean. *(Phaseolus limensis). See* Christmas lima.

Speckled lima bean. *(Phaseolus limensis). See* Christmas lima.

Split pea. *(Pisum sativum). See* Pea.

Steuben yellow-eye bean. Related to the kidney bean *(Phaseolus vulgaris). See* Yellow-eye bean.

Swedish brown bean. Related to the kidney bean *(Phaseolus vulgaris)*. Introduced by Swedish immigrants to northern states of the U.S. about 100 years ago.

Grown in Idaho and Sweden.

About ⅓-inch oval; mustard brown color, with color retained after soaking and cooking. Traditionally used in Swedish smorgasbords, but try seasoning these beans with Indian spices, or with cumin and coriander, finished with a small dollop of yogurt and chopped fresh cilantro.

Sold by specialty food stores.

Soak at least 4 hours or overnight; or quick-soak. Cook 1 to 1½ hours. Or pressure cook (soaked) 20 mins., (unsoaked) 25 mins.

Tepary bean. *(Phaseolus acutifolius, var. latifolius).*

Native to Western Mexico; cultivated for five thousand years in Central Mexico. Grown in arid regions of southwest U.S.

About $1/4$-inch long, flattish shape; generally white or tan brown, but can also be gold, black, or even speckled with navy blue. Color retained after soaking and cooking. Good flavor.

Sold in Hispanic markets or specialty food stores.

Soak at least 4 hours or overnight; or quick-soak. Cook 1 hour. Or pressure cook (soaked) 20 mins., (unsoaked) 25 mins.

Tongues of Fire bean. Related to the cranberry bean *(Phaseolus vulgaris).* Also called *borlotto lingua di fuoco.*

Grown in Idaho. Also cultivated in Italy and Latin America.

About $1/2$-inch long; beige mottled with brown. Color pales during soaking, but flavor is very fresh. Popular in Italian dishes.

Sold by specialty food stores.

Soak at least 4 hours or overnight; or quick soak. Cook 1 to $1^1/2$ hours. Or pressure cook (soaked) 20 mins., (unsoaked) 25 mins.

Turtle bean. Related to the kidney bean *(Phaseolus vulgaris). See* Black bean.

Whippoorwill bean.

Grown in Texas.

About $1/4$-inch long; medium brown color. Used in Southern cooking.

Sold by specialty food stores.

Soak at least 4 hours or overnight; or quick-soak. Cook 1 hour. Or pressure cook (soaked) 20 mins., (unsoaked) 25 mins.

White bean. Related to the kidney bean *(Phaseolus vulgaris)*. This group includes cannellini, Great Northern, haricot, *ingen mame*, navy, *soisson*, white kidney, white marrow, small white and Yankee beans.

Grown in California, Colorado, Idaho, Kansas and Washington. Also in Ethiopia, Mediterranean, South America, Turkey and the United Kingdom.

Of varying size, mostly $3/_8$-inch long; nutty flavor, classic for minestrone and for long slow baking. Available canned cooked, or dried.

Sold in most supermarkets.

Soak at least 4 hours or overnight; or quick-soak. Cook 1 to $1^1/_2$ hours. Or pressure cook (soaked) 25 mins., (unsoaked) 30 mins.

White runner bean. Related to the scarlet runner *(Phaseolus coccineus)*. *See* Runner bean.

Grown in California.

About $5/_8$-inch long, plump oval shape; ivory color; sweetish flavor. Makes a delicious vegetable side dish or soup ingredient.

Sold by specialty food stores.

Soak at least 4 hours or overnight; or quick-soak. Cook 1 to $1^1/_2$ hours. Or pressure cook (soaked) 25 mins., (unsoaked) 30 mins.

Winged bean. *(Psophocarpus tetragonolobus)*. Also called Goa bean, asparagus bean, four-angled bean, Manila bean and princess pea. Related to the soybean.

Origin: New Guinea and Southeast Asia. Grown in tropical areas such as Africa, East Indies, the Philippines, Southern India and Sri Lanka. Can be found in southernmost Florida, California and Texas.

Edible seeds, pods and tubers. Oil can be extracted from the bean-seed, similar to the soybean. Slice and cook pods as you would green string beans.

Sold in Asian markets.

Wren's Egg bean. Related to the cranberry bean *(Phaseolus vulgaris)*.

Grown in California.

About $3/8$-inch, plump and slightly globular; beige mottled with pink.

Sold by specialty food stores.

Soak at least 4 hours or overnight; or quick-soak. Cook about 1 hour. Or pressure cook (soaked) 20 mins., (unsoaked) 25 mins.

Yellow-eye bean. Related to the kidney bean *(Phaseolus vulgaris)*. Also called dot-eye bean, molasses-face bean and Yellow-eyed China bean.

Grown in California, Idaho and Michigan.

About $1/2$-inch, oval shaped; ivory white with mustard-yellow mark on the keel. Steuben Yellow-eye variety has more mustard color than white. Color retained after cooking. Mild flavor with mealy texture. Traditional in Maine for baked-bean dishes and stewing. Makes a light, colorful summer salad, tossed with finely diced carrots, celery, garlic, purple onion, parsley, tomato, fennel and olive oil.

Sold by specialty food stores.

Soak at least 4 hours or overnight; or quick-soak. Cook 45 mins to 1 hour. Or pressure cook (soaked) 25 mins., (unsoaked) 30 mins.

APPENDIX 2

Shopping Guide

Health-food stores, supermarkets, and specialty food stores offer many of the bean varieties described in this book. The following stores, ethnic markets and specialty ranches offer selections of unusual dried-bean varieties and bean products—and they accept mail orders. Write or telephone for catalog and prices before placing orders, since quantities of legumes are sometimes limited.

ARIZONA

Native Seeds/SEARCH
2509 N. Campbell Avenue, # 325
Tucson, Arizona 85719
(602) 327-9123
Unusual heirloom beans of Southwest U.S. and Northwest Mexico, for the home gardener and ready-to-eat. Ask for catalog ($1.00).

CALIFORNIA

Bazaar of India
1331 University Avenue
Berkeley, California 94702
(415) 548-4110

Bombay Bazaar
1034 University Avenue
Berkeley, California 94710
(415) 848-1671

Johnson Ranches
22154 Viola Avenue
Corning, California 96021
(916) 824-4537
Multi-flavored bean chips

House of Spices
5113 Mowry Avenue
Fremont, California 94536
(415) 791-8014
Indian dals and spices

Catalina's Market
1070 N. Western Avenue
Hollywood, California 90028
(213) 464-3595
*Nuña beans and other South
American varieties*

Luzann Food Imports
Pacific Village Plaza 2068-B
Pacific Coast Highway
Lomita, California 90717
(213) 325-1664
*Nuña beans and other South
American varieties*

Bezjian Groceries
4725 Santa Monica Boulevard
Los Angeles, California 90029
(213) 663-1503
Indian dals and spices

Mr. K's Gourmet Foods
and Coffees
Stall 430, Farmer's Market
Third and Fairfax
Los Angeles, California 90036
(213) 934-9117
Indian dals

Bombay Spiceland
8650 Reseda Boulevard, No. 4-5
Northridge, California 91324
(818) 701-9383
Indian dals and spices

G.B. Ratto & Company
821 Washington Street
Oakland, California 94607
(415) 832-6503, (800) 325-3483
FAX: (415) 836-2250
*Good selection of unusual beans and
lentils; retail and mail order. Ask
for price list.*

The Bean Bag
818 Jefferson Street
Oakland, California 94607
(415) 839-8988, FAX: (415) 791-0705
*A specialty food store with large
selection of unusual beans and
spices; wholesale, retail and mail
order. Ask for price list.*

La Colina Market
Hill Plaza
290 N. Hill Avenue
Pasadena, California 91109
(818) 568-1192
*Nuña beans and other South American
varieties*

Phipps Ranch
P.O. Box 349
Pescadero, California 94060
(415) 879-0787
*Large selection of unusual beans;
wholesale, retail and mail order.
Ask for price list.*

Haig's Delicacies
642 Clement Street
San Francisco, California 94118
(415) 752-6283

India Gifts and Food
643 Post Street
San Francisco, California 94109
(415) 771-5041
Indian dals and spices

Real Food Co.
1023 Stanyan Street
San Francisco, California 94117
(415) 564-2800

Real Food Co.
3939 24th Street
San Francisco, California 94114
(415) 282-9500

Real Food Co.
1234 Sutter Street
San Francisco, California 94109
(415) 474-8488

Broadway Deli
1457 Third Street Promenade
Santa Monica, California 90406
(213) 451-0616
*Unusual beans, papadini and
pappadums*

COLORADO

Adobe Milling Co., Inc.
P.O. Box 596
535 East Highway 666
Dove Creek, Colorado 81324
(303) 677-2620,   (800) 54-ADOBE
FAX: (303) 677-2667
*Anasazi® and bolita beans; wholesale,
    retail and mail order.*

CONNECTICUT

India Spice and Gift Shop
3295 Fairfield Avenue
Bridgeport, Connecticut 06605
(203) 384-0666

DISTRICT OF COLUMBIA

Casa Peña
1636 17th Street NW
Washington, D.C. 20009
(202) 462-2222
Mexican beans and spices

Spices and Foods Unlimited, Inc.
2018A Florida Avenue NW
Washington, D.C. 20009
(202) 265-1909

FLORIDA

Indian Grocery Store
2342 Douglas Road
Miami Beach, Florida 33134
(305) 448-5869

IDAHO

Good Taste
131 First Avenue North
P.O. Box 4569
Ketchum, Idaho 83340-4569
Tel and FAX: (208) 726-8881
(800) 424-8881
*A specialty food store with large
    selection of unusual beans;
    wholesale, retail and mail order.
    Ask for price list.*

ILLINOIS

Conte Di Savoia
555 West Roosevelt, #7
Chicago, Illinois 60607
(312) 666-3471

India Gifts and Foods
1031 West Belmont Avenue
Chicago, Illinois 60650
(312) 348-4392

India Groceries
5010 North Sheridan Road
Chicago, Illinois 60640
(312) 334-3351

Oriental Foods & Handicrafts, Inc.
3708 North Broadway
Chicago, Illinois 60613
(312) 248-8024

Supermercado Maria Cardenas
1714 West 18th Street
Chicago, Illinois 60608
(312) 666-2532
Dried fava beans

MARYLAND

Indian Super Bazaar
3735 Rhode Island Avenue
Mount Rainier, Maryland 20822
(301) 927-2224

Indian Sub-Continental Store
908 Philadelphia Avenue
Silver Spring, Maryland 20910
(301) 589-8417

Indian Emporium
68-48 New Hampshire Avenue
Takoma Park, Maryland 20012
(301) 270-3322

MASSACHUSETTS

India Tea and Spice, Inc.
453 Common Street
Belmont, Massachusetts 02178
(617) 484-3737

MICHIGAN

Gabriel Importing Co.
2461 Russell Street
Detroit, Michigan 48207
(313) 567-2890

India Grocers
35-46 Cass Avenue
Detroit, Michigan 48201
(313) 831-5480

MINNESOTA

International House of Foods
75 Island Avenue West
Minneapolis, Minnesota 55401
(612) 379-2335

MISSOURI

Quality International
3228 Ivanhoe
St. Louis, Missouri 63139
(314) 781-2444

Seema Enterprises
10612 Page Avenue
St. Louis, Missouri 63132
(314) 423-9990

NEW JERSEY

India Bazaar
204 Hudson Street
Hoboken, New Jersey 07030
(201) 653-8116

Bombay Bazaar
797 Newark Avenue
Jersey City, New Jersey 07306
(201) 963-5907

Krishna Grocery Store
103 Broadway
Passaic, New Jersey 07057
(201) 472-3025

NEW YORK

Beirut Groceries
199 Atlantic Avenue
Brooklyn, New York 11201
(212) 624-9615

Maharaj Bazaar
665 Flatbush Avenue
Brooklyn, New York 11225
(212) 941-2666

Sahadi Importing Company, Inc.
187 Atlantic Avenue
Brooklyn, New York 11201
(212) 624-4550

Patel Discount Center
74-17 Woodside Avenue
Elmhurst, New York 11373
(212) 478-4547

House of Spices
42-92 Main Street
Flushing, New York 11355
(212) 539-2214

America India Traders
139 Division Street
New York City, New York 10002
(212) 226-0467

Annapurna
127 East 28 Street
New York City, New York 10016
(212) 889-7540

Dean & DeLuca
560 Broadway
New York City, New York 10012
(212) 431-1691, (800) 221-7714
*A specialty food store with many
unusual beans and spices; retail
and mail order. Ask for price list.*

Foods of India
120 Lexington Avenue
New York City, New York 10016
(212) 683-4419

International Groceries
and Meat Market
529 Ninth Avenue
New York City, New York 10018
(212) 279-5514
Dried fava beans

Kalpana Indian Groceries
& Spices, Inc.
2528 Broadway
New York City, New York 10025
(212) 663-4190

Orient Export Trading Corporation
123 Lexington Avenue
New York City, New York 10016
(212) 685-3416

Thomas Zarras, Inc.
92 Reade Street
New York City, New York 10013
(212) 227-5278

OHIO

India Grocery
1568 North High Street
Columbus, Ohio 43085
(614) 291-0213

OKLAHOMA

Indian Foods and Spices
13125 East 36 Street
Tulsa, Oklahoma 74134
(918) 665-3184

OREGON

Porter's Foods Unlimited
125 West 11th Avenue
Eugene, Oregon 97401
(503) 342-3629

PENNSYLVANIA

Heirloom Seed Project
Landis Valley Museum
2451 Kissel Hill Road
Lancaster, Pennsylvania 17601
(717) 569-0401
*Unusual heirloom beans for the home
gardener. Ask for catalog ($2.00).*

House of Spices
716 West Wyoming Avenue
North Philadelphia, Penna. 19140
(215) 455-6870

House of Spices of New York
4101 Walnut Street
West Philadelphia, Penna. 19104
(215) 222-1111

Bombay Emporium
3343 Forbes Avenue
Pittsburgh, Pennsylvania 15213
(412) 682-4965

India Bazaar
3358 Fifth Avenue
Pittsburgh, Pennsylvania 15213
(412) 682-1172

India Foods
11619 Penn Hill Shopping Center
Pittsburgh, Pennsylvania 15235
(412) 242-9977

TEXAS

Yoga and Health Center
2912 Oaklawn Avenue
Dallas, Texas 75219
(214) 528-8681

Jay Store
4023 West Himier Street
Houston, Texas 77027
(713) 871-9270

VERMONT

Vermont Bean Seed Company
Garden Lane
Fair Haven, Vermont 05743-0250
(802) 2273-3400
*Unusual heirloom beans for the home
gardener. Ask for catalog.*

WASHINGTON

De Laurenti
    International Food Market
1435 First Avenue
Seattle, Washington 98101
(206) 622-0141

Specialty Spice House
Pike Place Market
Seattle, Washington 98105
(206) 622-6340

Buckeye Beans & Herbs
East 9514 Montgomery
Spokane, Washington 99206
(509) 926-9963, (800) 227-1686
*Seasoned mixes of beans and lentils for
soups and chili; wholesale, retail
and mail order.*

Specialty Spice House
Tacoma Mall
Tacoma, Washington 98049
(206) 474-7524

WISCONSIN

International House of Foods
440 West Gorham Street
Madison, Wisconsin 53703
(608) 255-2554

Chadda Imports
1450 East Brady Street
Milwaukee, Wisconsin 53202
(414) 277-1227

Indian Groceries and Spices
4807 West North Avenue
Milwaukee, Wisconsin 53208
(414) 445-9202

An Invitation

In order to keep the appendixes up to date and as complete as possible for future printings, the authors invite readers to share any further information they have about unusual bean varieties that are available in commercial quantities.

Please send full particulars about the beans, including details of where they are grown, where they may be purchased, how they can be cooked and served, and small samples, if possible, for identification. Readers' cooperation will be sincerely appreciated. Correspondence should be addressed to:

Kathleen Mayes and Sandra Gottfried
c/o Woodbridge Press Publishing Company
P.O. Box 6189
Santa Barbara, California 93160

Index to Recipes

Index